OTHER MEN'S HEROES

OTHER MEN'S
HEROES

Scots honoured on the world's stamps

ALWYN JAMES

I have made a posie of other men's flowers and nothing but the thread that binds them is mine own.

Montaigne

Thoughts of heroes were as good as warming-pans.

Meredith

MACDONALD PUBLISHERS • EDINBURGH
LOANHEAD • MIDLOTHIAN • SCOTLAND

To
Dad and Mam
who answered a boy's questions
and encouraged more

©Alwyn James 1982
Designed and edited by Jenny Carter

Published by
Macdonald Publishers
Loanhead, Midlothian EH20 9SY

ISBN 0904265 54 4

Printed in Scotland by
Macdonald Printers (Edinburgh) Limited
Edgefield Road, Loanhead, Midlothian EH20 9SY.

Contents

Introduction

'To seek out new worlds and new civilisations . . .
To boldly go where no man has gone before . . .'

There cannot be many people in the English-speaking world who have got through the 1970s without coming across the language's most celebrated split infinitive introducing "Star Trek," that long-running peep into the future through the log-books of the Star Ship *Enterprise*.

We are shown that in those distant days the nations have become internations, that the harmonious team manning, or rather personning, the space-ship, has been culled from all segments of this globe of ours. There is the black and voluptuous Uhura, the reliable and Slavonic Chekhov, the thoughtful and Oriental Sulu and, in case we have left out nations as yet unknown, there is the all-purpose Spock, offspring of a terrestrial mother and extra-terrestrial father.

So far so good, but when we come to look at the key people running the ship, more than a touch of racialism creeps in. The ship's leader, man of thought and action, is one James T. Kirk, about as Scottish a name as one could produce. On a long journey to strange and unpredicted environments the man of medicine is no less important, and here we have moved from the Lowlands of Scotland to the Highlands with the name McCoy. Coincidence, perhaps, so we progress to the next officer—the Chief Engineer, Montgomerie Scott, usually called Scottie and occasionally to be seen sporting an interesting tartan plaid during formal dinners.

There could be of course a simple explanation for the clutch of Caledonians running this ship of the future—the author may have been a Scot, the programme may be subsidised by the Scottish Tourist Board, the names may have been picked out of an old New York telephone directory.

I would like to believe that the Scottish names are a hangover from that astonishing period of around a century and a half, from about 1760 to around 1910 (although don't take either of those dates as rigid) when Scots tackled almost every aspect of human venture in which they were able "to seek out new worlds . . . to boldly go where no man had gone before," and achieved fame in virtually all of them. A nation that numbered around 1.3 million at that first date and had reached only 2.3 million by the end, led the world in a handful of activities, notably those represented by Kirk, Scottie and McCoy, namely exploration, soldiering, medicine, engineering and invention, but also including a few not represented aboard *USS Enterprise,* such as literature, economics, philosophy, politics and sport.

The breadth of that excellence in terms of geography, fields of endeavour and time span was brought home to me in a specific way early in 1980 when, in an attempt to try and rationalise some of the stamp collecting of my son Kevin, I suggested to him a number of thematic topics. Having run through the usual ones of space exploration, sports, birds, reptiles, I came up with "Famous Scots." He was singularly unimpressed, dismissing the suggestion with the finality— "There can't be many of those on stamps." Challenged, I went off to the local library and took out for the weekend the weighty 1740-page *Stamps of the World* by Stanley Gibbon. I adopted a fairly rigid definition. I would include only those people who considered themselves to be Scots or who were regarded by others as Scots. I have avoided going to second-generation Scots or beyond—as an indication of just what avenues that would open up, in Soviet stamps alone it would take in General Barclay de Tolly of the famous Aberdeen family, Lermontov the national poet whose family were originally Learmonths,

Edvard Grieg, sprung from the losing side at Culloden and Ernest Rutherford, New Zealand Scot of the second-generation taught by Scots of the first.

I have not included stamps on which Scots appear as "extras" to the main event being commemorated.

I have discounted those stamps which display items made by Scots, whether ships or cathedrals, Joan of Arc's banner or the bridge to link Buda to Pest. I have also ruled out stamps bearing objects which take their name from the Scots who discovered them—eliminating Forsythias and Gardenias, Grant's Antelope and Thomson's Gazelle and a host of flora, fauna and even bacteria.

Despite these restrictions, I was hooked and astounded. Surely no nation could match the sheer numbers and variety of the Scots found on postage stamps. My interest and admiration were aroused—and this book resulted.

It is not a stamp book, although I have included catalogue numbers for the stamp enthusiasts. It is, as the title suggests, a book about those Scots who have been honoured outside of their own country. Many writers have produced books on Famous Scots. This book is unique in that I have not made the selection myself; it has been made for me, by more than eighty nations over a period of more than seventy years. It includes people who perhaps would not be included in any home-made selection; it will exclude, glory be, many of the Scots who have been overpraised at home.

The biographies are brief and will, I hope, whet your appetite for more information (I have indicated where to look for some of it). Taken together I believe they will say something beyond the sum of the parts, something of the unique dynamism which existed in Scotland between 1760 and 1910, based firmly on two mainsprings: a great belief in the power of education and a great belief in humanity. Those values, along with an enthusiasm for all-round personal development and a conviction that problems were there to be solved, were carried from Scotland to a hundred host countries.

Acknowledgements

I would like to record a very special indebtedness to the following people who have made a contribution to any qualities this book might have:

Weir Gilmore, whose delightful little book *Great Scots*, gives a fine introduction to the wealth of Scotland's contribution to the world in terms of talented people.

Stanley Hunter of the Alba Stamp Group, whom I discovered too late to save me many months of stamp research and who has enough information on even the most oblique reference to Scots on the world's stamps to fill a couple more books. He will learn less than anyone from this book of mine, although he might find some pages of interest!

The Gorebridge Local History Society, who, by being on the receiving end of a rather lengthy evening of talk and slides on the theme of Other Men's Heroes, helped sharpen up some of these biographies.

A host of stamp dealers and librarians whose numbers in no way detract from the important individual contribution which each made and the help which they have given me.

Ian McLellan of the Clydesdale Bank for the careful attention he paid to the proposals relating to the sponsorship of this book—and of course to the Bank for its decision to go ahead with a style of involvement which was quite new for Scottish companies.

The stamp-issuing authorities of so many countries who gave permission for full-colour reproduction of the stamps in this book.

EXPLORERS & TRAIL BLAZERS

The old Indian answered the white man's questions as best he could but he was clearly puzzled. "What," he asked Alexander Mackenzie on the Scots' epic search for a route to the Pacific, "can be the reason that you are so particular and anxious in your enquiries of us respecting a knowledge of this country? Do you white men now know everything in the world?"

That Indian had spotted the symptoms—the endless questions, the presence of these strange white men in places where they did belong—but he had missed the reason for it all. It was not that the white men knew everything, but that they believed that everything *could* be known and that everything *should* be known. This curiosity, not untinged with considerations of fame, trade, wealth and power, lay behind the "expansion" of Europe into every other continent. The scouts of this expansion were the explorers and no nation was more prolific in the production of this specialist breed than Scotland.

Sanche de Gramont, writer and explorer, in his fine story of the Niger River, *The Strong Brown God*, list as examples of this "amazing output" Alexander Mackenzie, "Abyssinian" Bruce, Livingstone and, in the case of the Niger River alone Mungo Park, Gordon Laing, Hugh Clapperton and Dixie Denham. As you will see from this first section there are many more beside that could legitimately be included in that list.

"Why," asked de Gramont, "did a tiny nation, numbering in 1800 a mere 1,600,000 inhabitants produce so many explorers?"

He proceeds to give a full and perceptive answer, but if you look at these brief stories of some of Scotland's explorers the elements of the answer will emerge. As a poor country with a lengthy coastline, Scotland had a long tradition of trade with the countries of Europe and this tradition produced a nation ready and willing to go out to the new areas of the world as they were opened up for trade and settlement. The pressures at home—poverty, eviction, politics—may have produced

Scotland's long and continuing emigration, but the explorers often had something extra, some get-up-and-go ingredient. Some of them went off as young men to make a name for themselves in business—to the Hudson Bay Company or to the new colonies of Australia. Some joined the army and willingly went off to the frontiers of Empire. Some were driven not by economic misery but by a desire to take Christianity to the benighted lands.

The final ingredient which made Scotland the world's most prolific producer of explorers was education. Look at the men in this section and you will see that to them exploration and knowledge were inextricably bound up. Even when they were setting out with a particular goal in mind—a passage to the North-West, a link with the Pacific, a route through Australia—their explorations involved a considerable degree of work recording, identifying, describing and locating. This was no job for brave but uneducated adventurer. It was a task for the trained man, the intelligent man, the physically strong man, the dauntless man, for a type of man which Scotland, with its advanced and widespread education system, its acceptance of travel as a natural activity for any progressive adult and its frequent poverty, famine or persecution was in a unique position to provide.

Mungo Park 1771-1806

—finding the Niger— and drowning in it

At first sight there was nothing extraordinary in the Scottish Borders scene. The local lawyer, unable to find his young doctor friend at home, had gone off to a nearby stretch of water

and discovered him there, idly throwing stones into the
Yarrow. Dull and ordinary? Perhaps, until the young doctor
explained to his friends that it was by throwing stones in the
streams and counting the time it took for the bubbles to come to
the surface that he had been able to find out the best places to
cross all those streams in Africa and complete the most
astonishing exploration in history. And we know about the
incident because the young lawyer, Walter Scott, wrote about
it, along with tales of Mungo Park's nightmares, to show just
what forces led the young man, after his first amazing
achievement, to return to Africa for a second and fatal
expedition, telling Scott that "he would rather brave Africa
and all its horrors than wear out his life in long and toilsome
rides over the hills of Scotland, for which the remuneration was
hardly enough to keep body and soul together."

Mungo Park was born on 10 September 1770 on his father's
farm of Foulshiels on the banks of the Yarrow just above the
Borders town of Selkirk. The elder Mungo was a tenant farmer
on the lands of the Duke of Buccleuch, but frugal living and
hard work seems to have produced a reasonable family income
and he took care to educate the eight of his thirteen children
who got through the infant illnesses. Mungo junior went on to
the grammar school at Selkirk and at the age of fifteen,
encouraged by the example of his older brother Adam, decided
to study medicine. He became apprentice to a local surgeon
and in 1789 went to the University of Edinburgh, which was
beginning to establish itself as a world centre for the study of
medicine. No less significantly in the light of his later career,
Park at this time made a tour of the Highlands with his
botanist/gardener brother-in-law James Dickson.

Dickson, trained in the gardens of Traquair House, that
beautiful and still largely unchanged home outside
Innerleithen, had gone to London and made a name for himself
and become a friend of Sir Joseph Banks President of the Royal
Society and a would-be autocrat of British science. When
Mungo Park came to London to seek his fortune, Dickson

introduced him to the influential Banks and Park found himself as a ship's surgeon bound for the East Indies. He returned with a hoard of experiences and notes on eight exotic fish as yet unplotted by the enthusiasts of Britain. The Linnaeus Society heard his paper and published his findings.

Sir Joseph must have been pleased with the success of his raw protegé, for on 23 July 1794, the autocrat in his rôle of doyen of the African Association, appointed Mungo Park to go as "Geographical Missionary" to West Africa. The twenty-four-year-old Scot, undeterred by the knowledge that his predecessor in the post had set off in 1790, but after a year's worth of dispatches had disappeared without trace, left England without waiting for a proposed escort of fifty men and set sail for West Africa. He progressed up the Gambia river to the station of fellow Scot Dr John Laidley at Pisania and here the young doctor, laid low with fever, spent the time learning Mandingo and something of the land and people. After a few months he was ready for the great adventure, but perhaps a little blasé in his preparations. He set off with a Madingo guide/interpreter called Johnson, a slave called Demba, a horse and two asses. His baggage when compared with that of the other Scottish explorers in this section seemed inadequate. "My baggage was light, consisting chiefly of provisions for two days, a small assortment of beads, amber and tobacco for the purchaseof a fresh supply as I proceeded; a few changes of linen and other necessary apparel, an umbrella, a pocket sextant, a magnetic compass and a thermometer, together with two fowling pieces, two other pair of pistols and some other articles."

This first journey of Mungo Park's was to be one of the most miraculous in the story of European exploration. His quest was to find a river in a region of Timbuctu, without the benefit of knowing its mouth or its source, and indeed relying on only a few vague tales as to its course, or its very existence. He set off confidently on his search, an umbrella pacifying the first monarch he encountered. Further contacts were not so straightforward. Natives just came and helped themselves to the white man's property and when he reached Moorish territory, the Christian was fair game for any treatment that could be devised. At this stage his attendants wisely deserted him.

He was imprisoned by one desert king for two and a half months, during which the natives delighted in subjecting the poor explorer to a variety of humiliations. The least painful of the experiences came when a group of Moorish women wanted to find out whether or not the Christians practised circumcision. Mungo Park's knowledge of group psychology saved the day as he explained that it was not usual to give proof to so many women, but selected the youngest, prettiest and most blushing from among them. The rest left—and Park never had to give the "ocular demonstration."

The tall handsome scarecrow must have had some appeal left as the Queen of the leader urged her husband to release him. The Scot was turned out into the middle of a tribal war and managed to escape to the more friendly land of the Bambara. With a band of refugees he came, on 20 July 1796, to the Niger, not far from the town of Segou, he had found the middle section of the great river and established in which direction it flowed. The local ruler saw no benefit in keeping Park, as the man had nothing worth stealing and sent him away with a guide and 5000 cowrie shells. At this stage a little common sense entered the proceedings when Park's guide asked why Park had come at all this way to look at the river. "Are there no rivers in your own country and is not one river like another? That comment could replace the one made by the Red Indian to Mackenzie quoted at the beginning of this section.

Park set off along the Niger to find Timbuctu and perhaps the termination of the Niger. His misfortunes mounted. He ran out of the cowrie shell currency, was starving, quivering with fever, drained of energy, attacked as a spy, and set upon by robbers. Not surprisingly, his resolve began to falter. "I sat down for some time looking around me with amazement and terror. Whichever way I turned nothing appeared but danger and difficulty. I saw myself in the midst of a vast wilderness in the depth of the rainy season; naked and alone; surrounded by savage animals and men still more savage. I was 500 miles from the nearest European settlement."

He pressed on, now with the advantage of more friendly natives (they even got back some of his stolen clothes!), poverty so abject that he was no longer a target for thieves and a sallow complexion and long beard that gave him the look of an Arab. On 10 June 1797, in the company of a slave-dealer, Park arrived back at the point near Pisania at which his travels had begun. The eighteen months had been crammed with adventure and incident such as no African explorer could match—and priceless information about the size and course of the great Niger. Park returned to Britain and, from the notes made on scraps of papers and kept in his hat, he set about producing the finest of all the journals of African exploration.

He returned speedily to Scotland after a spell of lionisation in London, the main attraction being the daughter of his old surgeon master, soon to become his wife.

Settling back slowly into the life and tempo of the Borders, Mungo Park became a local practitioner, made friends with his lawyer neighbour, Walter Scott, and was, after a few years, to be found lobbing pebbles in the Yarrow and dreaming of a return to Africa, bitten by the bug of exploration, but also smouldering with resentment and hatred for his treatment by the Moors.

This time the expedition was to be a large one, Government-backed and prepared for trouble, manned by ex-convicts and deserters in return for their freedom. The journey did not begin until 1805 and the party set off into the interior in April of that year. Park, the arch-loner and brilliant individualist, found an entirely different set of problems attached to his new expedition. Dysentery swept through the party, some men got lost and barely a quarter of the original party remained when Park reached the Niger on 19 August; a month later they were at Segou. Three months were spent there before Park, determined to press on, set off by river on two mouldering canoes patched into a single vessel.

The rest of the Mungo Park story is dark and confused. What is reasonably certain is that the explorer, this time on the offensive and firing at any signs of aggression from the river bank, managed to make some 1500 miles along the river and get to within 600 miles of the point where it discharges into the Gulf of Guinea, before the boat was ambushed and the party wiped out at the Bussa rapids. The stamps issued by The Gambia in 1971 to commemorate the 200th aniversary of Park's birth depict this final scene, along with Mungo Park in a dug-out canoe and Mungo Park among the hills of his native Borders homeland.

Alexander Mackenzie 1764-1820

—a strand to link a nation

Something about the dancing Indian children caught Alexander Mackenzie's eye: their earrings. He peered at them carefully—they were coins, British George III halfpennies and some 1787 coins from the State of Massachusetts Bay. They could not have originated from the direction he had come, from the east over the northernmost reaches of the Rockies; they must have come from the west. Were they evidence of a chain of trading links between this Indian tribe and the European traders on the Pacific coast? If so, Mackenzie saw the fulfilment of his goal—to blaze a trail from the settlements of the east to the shores of the western ocean.

He had begun this particular voyage from Fort Chipewyan on the banks of Lake Athabasca on the very north-west fringe of settled Canada. He was there as a fur trader. The trading post had been set up by Mackenzie and his cousin Roderick in 1788. Alexander, born in 1764 in one of the most remote corners of Scotland, near Stornoway, chief town of the "Long Isle," had come to Canada at the age of sixteen and he joined the firm of Gregory McLeod & Co, working first in their Montreal counting house, then moving on to the trading post at Detroit and finally to Churchill River country. When the firm amalgamated with North-West Fur, a new rival to the Hudson Bay Company, he was made a partner.

From his base at the trading post at Fort Chipewyan, Mackenzie became convinced that there would be a route through to the west coast. No-one had at that time succeeded in crossing the American continent north of Mexico.

The results of Mackenzie's first exploration were summed up in the name he gave to the great river which he discovered: the River of Disappointment. On 3 June 1789, he set off with four French Canadians, a German named John Steinbruch and an Indian guide. The party paddled by canoe down the Slave River to the Great Slave Lake and then down a river to the north. The river, which would one day bear the name of Mackenzie, carried them to a great expanse of water. Small whales and an undeniable tide which nearly carried the baggage away convinced Mackenzie that this was the sea, but he was equally sure that he had found not the Pacific but a northern coast of Canada. He returned to Chipewyan after a round trip of nearly 3000 miles in 120 days.

In May 1793, he set out once more, this time with a larger party of seven British and French settlers and two Indian guides. "The canoe was put into water," he recorded, "her dimensions were 25 feet long within, exclusive of the curves of stem and stern, 26 inches hold and 4 ft 9 inches beam. At the same time she was so light that two men could carry her on a good road three or four miles without resting. In this slender vessel we shipped provisions, goods for presents, arms, ammunition and baggage to the weight of 3000 lb." It is interesting to compare this collection of impedimenta with the optimistic supplies which Mungo Park felt necessary for his voyage.

The "good road" which Mackenzie mentions was nowhere to be found so perhaps his estimate of a three mile stint for carrying the canoe becomes irrelevant. After the Slave River and the Great Slave Lake, Mackenzie followed the Peace River into the snow-capped mountains which had to be penetrated if the party was ever to reach the Pacific. They found themselves fighting upward into the mountain pass, dragging the canoe up fast flowing currents, hacking a path through dense forest, hauling the baggage up steep rocky faces. All the time, Mackenzie was hard at work making full notes on the features of the landscape to help later developers—where a road might be opened up, where a factory could be established, where a farm might thrive.

The party eventually reached the Great Divide, the high land where the rivers are born and decided to go westward to the Pacific or eastward to the plains. Eventually Mackenzie found one of the westward-flowing rivers and set off on the downward leg. Holding the canoe back proved to be no easier than pushing and pulling it upwards. On one occasion the party had to haul the canoe on a three-mile portage and took fourteen hours to do it. Eventually they came to an Indian village and it was here that Mackenzie spotted those coins in the earrings and became convinced that he was within striking distance of the Pacific. The voyage was far from finished, but on 17 July the group of men came to the banks of the Bella Coola and, helped by salmon and a canoe from some friendly Indians (the original canoe had been cached higher up for the return journey), they made the last lap down to Queen Charlotte Sound.

Mackenzie described how they "took possession of a rock where there was not space for more than twice our number and

which admitted defending ourselves with advantage." The party slept there and in the morning Mackenzie "mixed up some vermilion in melted grease and inscribed in large characters on the South East face of the rock on which we slept last night this brief memorial:
'Alexander Mackenzie from Canada by land, 22 July 1793'."

Mackenzie published a full account of his voyages in 1795, with a wealth of information which proved invaluable to the generation that was to come behind. He was knighted for his achievements in 1802 and in 1808 returned to his native Scotland, to Avoch House on the Black Isle. He died at Moulinearn near Pitlochry on 11 March 1820. One hundred and fifty years later Canada issued a postage stamp, bearing not a likeness of the explorer but a symbol of his achievement— the rock and the inscription which marked the spot where he proved that east and west *could* meet.

John McDouall Stuart 1815-1866

—doing a Mackenzie down-under

Whether you are building a web, a bridge or a nation, the spinning of the first thread to join the extremities is a crucial operation. In the construction of Canada, the first man to make that link to which all future threads would cling was Alexander Mackenzie: on the other side of the world, a fellow Scot, John McDouall Stuart, undertook a similar task—to find an all-season route which would link the southern coasts of Australia with the tropical shores of the north.

Stuart arrived in Adelaide in 1839, a twenty-three-year-old, born in Dysart on the northern shore of the Forth, educated in Edinburgh and fortified with a grounding in civil engineering in Glasgow. At this time, South Australia was being hailed as an exciting, new-style colony, being developed not as a receptacle for Britain's criminals but as a land of promise for her young men and women, her brave new world.

Stuart could hardly have had in mind the mighty mission with which he was to make his name, but providentially he started off his Australian life with the right decision for a future explorer; he became a surveyor's labourer.

Working on the fringes of a remote colony meant a hard camp life for the young man and a hasty indoctrination into the far-from-gentle art of bushmanship, living rough Australian-style, on two shillings and tenpence a day plus rations.

After five years of this life, yet another providential decision went Stuart's way when he was appointed as draughtsman on an expedition with the famous Australian trail-blazer, Captain Charles Sturt. The Sturt party left Adelaide in August 1844 to a heroes' send-off and returned in 1846 to an even noisier homecoming, having travelled well into the hot dusty interior of Australia and got beyond the half-way point to the northern coast. Stuart had aquired a clear understanding and admiration for Sturt's style of leadership and exploration. He had set out as a draughtsman and returned as an embryo explorer.

It was to be a dozen years before Stuart could put the lessons he learnt from Captain Sturt to good use. In 1858, he led a 1500-mile round trip into the interior, the first of a series of expeditions which established him as Australia's leading explorer. They laid down and hardened the pattern of this exploration technique: preparation, speed, toughness and observation.

As one biographer put it, Stuart saw "adventures" as a sign of incompetence. Preparation could reduce and eliminate them. He learnt with every trip and in his later expeditions the "adventures" were few and far between. He was perhaps the only major explorer never to have lost a man.

Speed was essential to any Australian explorer in view of the unreliability of water supplies. Thirst was to Stuart what the cold was to the Rosses, the mountains to Mackenzie and the jungle to Livingston. Horses were his answer—the camel was as yet an unproved alternative in central Australia—and he was among the first to dispense with the slow, laden drays in favour of speedier horse caravans.

Toughness was as important as speed and here Stuart's physical durability was almost legendary, until, sapped by years of travel, his final successful attempt to cross the continent saw him below his own high standards of fitness but still able to endure twelve hours in the saddle each day.

To those three characteristics, Stuart added another which was almost to be the hall-mark of the Scottish explorer; an unshakable feeling of responsibility to chart, log and detail everything that he could, for its own sake and for the benefit of those who were to follow behind. Not for Stuart the quick dash through the centre to chalk up a first. He undertook on his great voyage dozens of "branch explorations," setting off on two-day or four-day round trips according to what water was available and naming, mapping and noting what he saw. One aspect of this was his passion for naming features and his appetite for searching for suitable people to honour in this way. When he had honoured dignitaries and those financing his trips, he began to name places after friends, relatives, friends of relatives and relatives of friends and even—and it would be interesting to know if any other explorers were reduced to this—naming features after two of the horses on the expedition!

On 25 October 1861, John MacDouall Stuart set off on his sixth and what was to be his great climactic expedition. It did not begin in the most auspicious manner. The leader tried to calm down a horse overexcited by the Adelaide crowds, and was kicked unconscious; as he lay on the ground, the horse stamped on his hand and broke two joints of the first finger.

Fortunately, this was merely a ceremonial starting point and Stuart was able to join the main party north of Adelaide at Chambers Creek on the last day of the year. The Great Northern Expedition set off in earnest on 8 January 1862, ten men and seventy-one horses. The men were for the most part youngsters; one old lady at Arkaba had been pessimistic: "I am sure such a lot of beardless boys will never be able to cross the continent and we shall never see them back again." If beards were an essential to good exploration, she may have taken some consolation from the leader's fine growth.

The drive to the north was long and arduous, the super-drought of that particular summer causing all sorts of problems as far as locating water supplies was concerned. Stuart never veered from his habit of going off to explore land alongside the main route. He was still as much a surveyor as an explorer. Natives varied from the friendly, providing some welcome cabaret, to the belligerent—setting fire to scrub so that breezes blew thick smoke in the eyes of the explorer and covered the aborigines' attacks. And often, even more dangerous, a combination of friendship and downright malevolence. The horses stood up well to the task and, with McGorrey, the smith, setting something of a record fitting and putting on seventy-three horse shoes in a day without a forge, gave continued service to the band.

For weeks, distant horizon succeeded distant horizon, but in July, John McDouall Stuart completed the last few miles of his mission and came to the wash of waters that was his goal. "I immediately dismounted, walked into the water or rather dipped my feet in the Indian Ocean as I promised Sir Richard McDonnell I would do if I had the chance." The ceremonial completion of the historic trek tied in with the ceremonial leaving of Adelaide, but with no recalcitrant horse to spoil matters this time. On 25 July between 11 a.m. and noon, the party remembered the lunch they had had at the Chambers' home in Adelaide exactly nine months earlier and hoisted the flag that had been made for them by Miss Elizabeth Chambers "the Union Jack with my name sewn in the centre of it." Stuart had crossed the centre of the continent, done it in style and logged the route so well that it was to form the exact basis of future development including the line followed by the Overland Telegraph.

The journey back was a harsh one for Stuart. His years of arduous living began to take their toll, he was stricken by fever, underwent violent fits of vomiting and had to be lifted into his saddle. He had undertaken six difficult journeys in just over four and a half years, spending a total of three and a half years away from civilisation. It was little to be wondered that he felt himself "in the grip of death." He made it back to Adelaide where news of the returning mission did much to dispel the gloom caused by the recently revealed story of the deaths of Burke and Wills on their ill-fated attempt. The streets were hung with tartan and the Scot was at the high point of his career.

Stuart lived for less than four years longer. Disillusioned with the lack of reward and by the haggling over his achievement, he returned to Scotland and then went to live in the south of England. He died in London on 4 June 1866 and was buried at Kensal Green Cemetery.

James Chalmers 1841-1901

—a missionary among cannibals

At a Sunday-school in the small village of Inveraray, a teacher read out to the class a letter from a missionary working in Fiji. The letter transformed the life of one of the pupils, fifteen-year-old James Chalmers, then working in a local lawyer's office. He decided that he wanted to become a missionary—and, even more specifically, a missionary in the South Seas.

Born at Ardrishaig in 1841, near the northernmost of the narrow necks of the Kintyre peninsula, James was the son of a local stonemason and received his education at a number of local schools in Ardrishaig, nearby Lochgilphead and Glen Aray. He now began to study religious subjects and in 1861 was accepted by Glasgow City Mission. Still determined to work in the South Seas, he joined the London Missionary Society and spent time at the Society's colleges preparing for the call. He was eventually accepted as a Congregational Missionary and in 1865, after a good grounding in the native tongue, he set foot in Rarotonga, one of the largest islands in the scattered Cook archipelago.

For ten years, he carried out a dedicated and patient ministry among peaceful and friendly natives. In 1876, he moved on to the much more unpredictable territory of New Guinea. His energy was impressive. In 1878, he visited more than one hundred native villages, in ninety of which he was the first white man ever to be seen. He realised, as other missionaries had done and were to do, that exploration was an essential part of his task and he undertook over seven years a brave and meticulous exploration of the Gulf of Papua.

The missionary-explorer also had the touch of the politician in him and, fearful of the effects of being ruled by Queensland, he lobbied to have the area made into a British Protectorate. In 1884, this was formally established with the arrival of Commander Erskine at Port Moresby. Chalmers, unidentified, would almost certainly feature on the postage stamp showing the hoisting of the flag (Papua 1934). On the companion stamp showing the official party aboard the *HMS Nelson* commanded by Erskine, Chalmers appears third from the left at the back.

Chalmers was responsible for organising the event and for gathering together chiefs from all over the area to meet Erskine on his arrival. After some well-earned leave, Chalmers travelled extensively, meeting—and impressing—Stevenson in Samoa.

In 1892, Chalmers returned to his task of bringing Christianity to the natives of New Guinea and tackled the more dangerous tribes of the mangrove swamps. He avoided death but not adventure until 1901, when the magnetic zeal of the indefatigable missionary came to an abrupt and gruesome end. Visiting a new part of the territory he went ashore at Goaribari Island hoping to pacify aggressive natives. He was murdered and devoured along with his fellow missionary, Oliver Tomkins.

James Clark Ross 1800-1862

—his compass pointed straight down

For nearly eight hundred years, since Italian sailors first learnt that a floating magnetised needle could tell them the direction of North when clouds hid the sun, navigators have relied on that bobbing compass needle for the practice of their complex craft. On 1 June 1831, James Clark Ross, a thirty-one-year-old naval commander, became the first of those navigators to stand on a spot where his compass needle pointed vertically downwards—the Magnetic Pole. He claimed the unprepossessing plot in the name of His Britannic Majesty William IV. In less patriotic vein, the peninsula on which it stood had already been named Boothia after the backer of the expedition—and the celebrated London gin is unlikely to get a better return from any of its modern sponsorships.

Reaching and confirming the Magnetic Pole (at that time the point was 70°5′17″ North and 96°46′45″ West but it has now moved several hundred miles away) was only one of a host of achievements of the great voyage, which began on 29 May 1829 at Woolwich and ended on 18 October 1833 in the Humber, and was commanded by James Ross's uncle, John Ross. The expedition had not located the elusive North-West Passage, but it had charted expansive tracts of the Arctic, established new features and confirmed or disproved the existence of earlier vaguely sketched outlines. Perhaps the most outstanding performance by the Rosses and their men was to spend four and a half years on a single voyage, including four winters locked in the Arctic ice.

James Clark Ross had been born probably in London but possibly in Wigtownshire in 1800, his father, eldest son of the Reverend Andrew Ross, having left Scotland for the metropolis to win fame and fortune as an entrepreneur. Any danger that the young James would become anglified and alienated from his Galloway roots was averted by his Uncle John, who had remained behind in the family haunts and was building the foundations of a naval career. He took a keen interest in his nephew and at the age of eleven the young lad joined his uncle's ship and was to serve under him for the next six years. In 1818, John Ross was given command of his first Arctic voyage in the quest for the North-West Passage which was to occupy the attentions of a number of restless navy officers in the doldrum years after Trafalgar.

The first voyage introduced the young midshipman James Ross to the never-changing hazards of such exploration: the inescapable cold which permitted stunted Arctic trees to resist and even break the stoutest axes; the great problems of finding food in the long winters (on one occasion the party found the dogs eating a sledge—only to discover that it had been made of frozen fish by the imaginative Eskimos); the new challenges which bergs and pack-ice introduced to ship handling; and the confused disorientation caused by the firm belief that a North-

West Passage existed and the abundant evidence that it did not.

James took to the life with increasing vigour, eagerly tackling the problems of navigation, scientific observation and sheer survival. That first expedition ended in controversy with the older Ross, as commander, winning the eternal enmity of the influential Admiralty Secretary John Barrow and being effectively excluded from any Royal Navy explorations as a result of the bitter slanging match that developed.

James, however, escaped the fate and, while his uncle fretted and fumed on the shores of Loch Ryan, building his fine home, North West Castle, today extended as a hotel, he took part in no fewer than four voyages with the explorer Parry. In all these explorations, there was a high scientific content, for the new wave of travellers were no longer looking for the treasure highway to Cathay and the Spice Islands that their predecessors of the sixteenth and seventeenth centuries had sought. James Ross revelled in this element, collecting and working on specimens of flora and fauna, becoming an accomplished taxidermist and discovering a very lovely gull which was to be named after him.

When John Ross eventually emerged from the backwaters to lead a new expedition to the Arctic, he was able to take with him a nephew who had overtaken him in experience of coming to terms with the polar environment. This new expedition was to be the first to make use of steam—the *Victory* was a sailing vessel equipped with a steam engine and paddles, which in the event turned out to be more useful in terms of publicity than propulsion.

The 1829-33 expedition did not prise open the North-West Passage, but did, by any standards, prove a success. The return to Britain of a party which everyone had given up for dead brought fame to them all, a knighthood to John Ross and promotion to James Ross.

James Ross found that his next project was one to keep him busy nearer home—and a welcome relief and recuperation after the strain and exhaustion of the long Arctic winters. He was put in charge of the first systematic magnetic survey of the British Isles. This developed into a wider study which eventually led Ross from the Arctic where he had made his name to the other end of the globe.

In the study of terrestrial magnetism patterns, the high latitudes in the southern hemisphere were in particular need of investigation and in James Ross, Britain had a ready-made leader, unequalled in polar experience or magnetism survey work. On 8 April 1839, he received his commission to *HMS Erebus* which was to undertake the expedition along with *HMS Terror*. The two vessels, each of around 350 tons, were sturdy ships strengthened for the expected challenge of the ice. The four voyages of the vessels, the last explorations of any note to be undertaken totally under sail, opened up the continent of Antarctica in a spectacular manner. Discoveries included Victoria Land, the Ross Sea, McMurdo Sound and the breathtaking Ross Ice Barrier. The only disappointment for Ross came when he was unable to get to the Magnetic Pole, an achievement which would have provided a symmetry to his attainment in the Arctic and appealed to the scientist in him. His work in the southern hemisphere is commemorated in the stamps of both British and French Antarctic Territories.

James came back to honours, rest and a marriage. And that rest looked like being a real one this time, as his new wife's family had written into the marriage contract an undertaking that he was to desist from polar exploration. The only release from that promise came when, with his wife's permission, he set off, as many others did, in vain search for the doomed Franklin expedition to the Arctic. Incidentally, the redoubtable John Ross was among the last to persevere with the quest, undertaking a search at the age of seventy-three. Despite the twenty-three-year gap in age, both Rosses covered an identical span of polar exploration from that first trip together in 1818 to the final searches for Franklin.

Sir John died in London on 30 August 1856, participating

fully in the deliberations of various scientific bodies right up to the end. His nephew James died six years later, having spent his retirement in Aylesbury.

James Clark Ross was the epitome of Victorian exploration: the talented, capable explorer, equally at home harpooning a whale, identifying a sea-bird (he was elected as a Fellow of the Linnaeus Society), quelling a mutiny, shooting a polar bear, fighting gales or pack-ice or making scientific readings and observations. He and his uncle have been strangely neglected by writers and historians although the world map is sprinkled with the name Ross in association with almost every geographical feature one could think of.

Alistair Forbes-Mackay 1878-1914

—rounding off the James Clark Ross story

On 16 January 1909, nearly seventy-eight years after James Clark Ross had stood at the Magnetic North Pole, explorers made it to the Magnetic South Pole. Ross had dearly wanted to complete the polar double and failed to do so, although in reaching his southern limit, he established a record which was to stand for fifty-eight years. The successful team did, however, contain one Scot among the three people who made it to the Magnetic South Pole and who are depicted on the stamp issued by Australian Antarctic Territories in 1959 to mark the fiftieth anniversary of the event. He was Alistair Forbes-Mackay.

Born on 27 February 1878 at Carskey in Argyllshire, the son

of a prosperous landowning family, Alistair Forbes-Mackay had a vigorous and adventurous start to his working life. He served as a trooper in South Africa with Baden-Powell's Police and then joined the Royal Navy as a ship's surgeon. The combination of man of action and of medicine won him a place on Shackleton's Expedition to Antarctica in 1908-1909 and he played an important part in the achievements of the great Irish explorer's venture.

Mackay had two especially significant roles. Firstly, the expedition was tackling the problem of traversing great tracts of the frozen continent by using for the first time Manchurian ponies: Mackay was the expert chosen to break and handle the ponies in the frightening conditions aboard ship and on the ice. Secondly, he was the second surgeon on the expedition and this was certainly no sinecure as one member of the team, injured with a flying block had to have his eye removed while another suffering from frost bite had to have some toes amputated.

Hardly less important was Mackay's great toughness and strength. He was a member of the three men chosen to ascend the active volcano Erebus, named after James Clark Ross's ship, and to determine its altitude—at 13,360 ft! The same team of the Welshman Edgeworth David, Australia's leading geographer and fifty years old, the Australian lecturer Douglas Mawson and the tough Scot was selected to make the attempt to reach the Magnetic South Pole. In view of important geophysical observations and measurements which were involved the two scientists were essential. Mackay provided essential medical experience and the muscle-power for the long uphill drive to the spot, 7000 ft above sea-level— and this at the end of a 1260 mile haul.

Early in 1909, the trio reached the Magnetic South Pole and, aided by a piece of string, were able to take a photograph of themselves on the very spot. Dr Alistair Forbes-Mackay appears on the right of the photograph. His career as a polar explorer was cut short five years later, when he was lost on Stefansson's Arctic Expedition.

nada 8

$2.5

Officer, 93rd (Sutherland Highlanders) Regiment of Foot, 1830

MO.

भारत
india

35

स्कॉटिश चर्च कालेज, कलकत्ता
SCOTTISH CHURCH COLLEGE, CALCUTTA

1980

EL SIRIUS - 1838

0.95 PTA
GUINEANA

REPUBLICA DE GUINEA ECUATORIAL

COMMEMORANT L'EXPLORATION DE L'AFRIQUE PAR STANLEY ET LIVINGSTONE

7 F

REPUBLIQUE DU BURUNDI

COMMEMORANT L'EXPLORATION DE L'AFRIQUE PAR STANLEY ET LIVINGSTONE

POSTE AERIENNE

18 F

REPUBLIQUE DU BURUNDI

COMMEMORANT L'EXPLORATION DE L'AFRIQUE PAR STANLEY ET LIVINGSTONE

27 F

POSTE AERIENNE

REPUBLIQUE DU BURUNDI

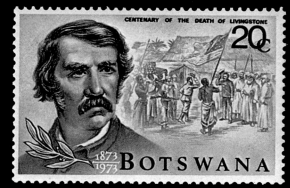

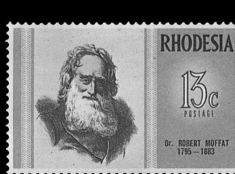

JOHN HANCOCK

1776
~
1976

JOSEPH HEWES

JOSIAH BARTLETT

United States
of
America
Bicentennial
AIRMAIL
T$1·00
TONGA

JOHN WITHERSPOON

STEPHEN HOPKINS

1776
~
1976

ELBRIDGE GERRY

JAMES WILSON

United States
of America
Bicentennial
POSTAGE
75s
TONGA

FRANCIS HOPKINSON

ABERDEEN ANGUS

URUGUAY $15

RURAL AMERICA

U.S. 8c

1873-1973 ANGUS CATTLE

PARAGUAY

correo

Gs.0.20

3p FALKLAND ISLANDS

Le curling
Curling

CANADA

6

7 Australia

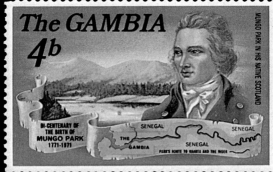

The GAMBIA
4b

MUNGO PARK IN HIS NATIVE SCOTLAND

BI-CENTENARY OF THE BIRTH OF MUNGO PARK 1771-1971

SENEGAL
SENEGAL
THE GAMBIA
SENEGAL
PARK'S ROUTE TO KAARTA AND THE NIGER

The GAMBIA
25b

TRAVELLING BY DUG-OUT CANOE

BI-CENTENARY OF THE BIRTH OF MUNGO PARK 1771-1971

SENEGAL
SENEGAL
THE GAMBIA
SENEGAL
PARK'S ROUTE TO KAARTA AND THE NIGER

The GAMBIA
37b

DEATH OF MUNGO PARK—BUSA RAPIDS—1806

BI-CENTENARY OF THE BIRTH OF MUNGO PARK 1771-1971

SENEGAL
SENEGAL
THE GAMBIA
SENEGAL
PARK'S ROUTE TO KAARTA AND THE NIGER

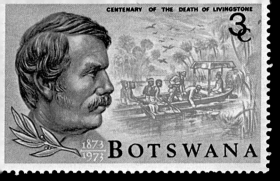

CENTENARY OF THE DEATH OF LIVINGSTONE

3C

1873
1973

BOTSWANA

100th
ANNIVERSARY OF
DAVID LIVINGSTONE'S
DEATH

CENTENARY OF THE DEATH OF Dr. LIVINGSTONE, 1813-1873

4n "Blessed are they... Zambia

THE DEATH OF Dr. LIVING

CENTENARY OF

15n Serving mankind Za

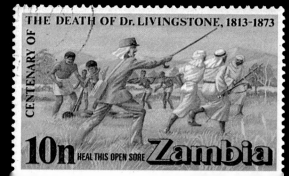

CENTENARY OF THE DEATH OF Dr. LIVINGSTONE, 1813-1873

10n HEAL THIS OPEN SORE Zambia

CENTENARY OF THE D

3n

MALAŴI
15 t

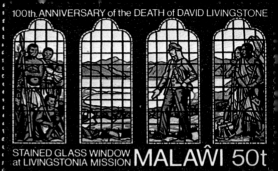

100th ANNIVERSARY of the DEATH of DAVID LIVINGSTONE

STAINED GLASS WINDOW
at LIVINGSTONIA MISSION MALAŴI 50t

1813-1873

bia

THE DEATH OF Dr. LIVINGSTONE, 1813-1873

CENTENARY OF

9n Exploration: Mosi-oa-Tunya
- Victoria Falls. Zambia

F Dr. LIVINGSTONE, 1813-1873

e, I presume... Zambia

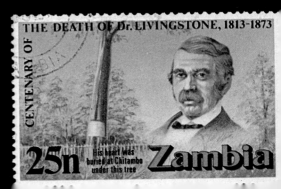

THE DEATH OF Dr. LIVINGSTONE, 1813-1873

CENTENARY OF

25n His heart was
buried at Chitambo
under this tree Zambia

REPUBLIQUE DU MALI
1881-1955
Sir Alexander Fleming
150F
POSTE AERIENNE 1975
COMBET

POPULAIRE DU CONGO
POSTES 1975
REPUBLIQUE
60F
ALEXANDER FLEMING · 1881·1955 ·

REPUBLIQUE POPULAIRE DU BENIN
POSTES 1978
50° Anniversaire de la DECOUVERTE DES ANTIBIOTIQUES
POMMADE SPECIMEN
FLEMING 1881-1955
300F
A.ASSOUTO
EDILA

U.N.
W.H.O
25
ANNIVERSARY
1948 - 1973
Sir ALEXANDER FLEMING
POSTAGE
LIBERIA
25c

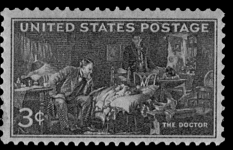

1881 · ALEXANDER FLEMING · 1955

DECOUVERTE DE LA PENICILLINE

GUILLAME

POSTE AERIENNE

101 F

RF

WALLIS ET FUTUNA

50th ANNIVERSARY OF THE DISCOVERY OF PENICILLIN
The problem of infection: World War I
20c
Mauritius

50th ANNIVERSARY OF THE DISCOVERY OF PENICILLIN
The first mould-growth: 1928
Re1
Mauritius

50th ANNIVERSARY OF THE DISCOVERY OF PENICILLIN
'Penicillium notatum'
Mauritius Rs1⁵⁰

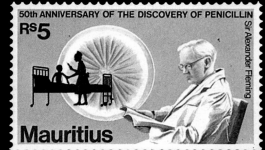

50th ANNIVERSARY OF THE DISCOVERY OF PENICILLIN
Rs5
Sir Alexander Fleming
Mauritius

Thomas Livingstone Mitchell 1792-1855

—the very model of a Scottish all-rounder

In 1853, aboard a boat returning to England, was the soldier-surveyor-explorer, Sir Thomas Livingstone Mitchell. He was making the trip in order to patent his new design for a screw-propellor for steam vessels. He whiled away the time translating for publication *The Lusiad* of Camoës, the great Portuguese classic. It would be difficult to imagine a more balanced example of the type of all-round talent which Scotland consistently succeeded in producing in her Golden Age.

Thomas Livingstone Mitchell was born at Craigend near Stirling on 16 June 1792. At sixteen he joined the army and served with some distinction in the Peninsular War, present at many of the great battles in Wellington's campaign and picking up a silver medal for bravery.

He returned after the war to put to use his talents as a surveyor and sketcher of military positions, preparing records and material to enable the authorities back home to indulge in action replays on the Whitehall desks. He left the army in 1826 as a major and the following year sailed to New South Wales to take up the post of assistant surveyor-general, rising after a brief spell to surveyor-general. The role was to take up his energies for the next quarter of a century.

His initial responsibility was for the development of new roads in the colony. His talent and work-rate were extraordinary. He surveyed a route for the road to link the West Plains with Bathurst. The proposals were turned down— today they are followed almost exactly for the road and rail link.

C

In 1831, he started on the type of work which was to convert him almost imperceptibly from a surveyor into an explorer. A recaptured convict told a cock-and-bull tale of an impressive river, navigable and flowing to the northern seas. Mitchell set off in search of this ready-made "road" and although he did not manage to find it, he did some valuable exploration before two members of his party were killed by aborigines. He was to carry out, over the next fifteen years or more, a valuable exploration of the hinterland of the established coastal settlements and in particular to discover what he called "Australia Felix," "Blessed or Happy Australia" thus opening up a rich and fertile part of Australia to sheep and cattle farming. The stamps depicting his achievements show Mitchell, together with woolly and horned symbols of what his discoveries meant to Australia.

His expeditions were usually undertaken with a team of rough and intractable convicts and the success of the travels says much for Mitchell's courage, imperious mien and leadership.

He was knighted in 1840 and died in October 1855.

Robert Moffat 1795-1883

— missionary for half a century

Robert Moffat had a better reason than most fathers-in-law to feel a little jealous of the man who married his daughter. Moffat, in terms of service to Africa, chalked up around fifty years, a record which few if any could approach—a record which his devoted wife shared with him.

Moffat, the great Moses-like patriarch of European missionaries in Africa, had the misfortune as far as fame is concerned of having to contend with the dazzling career of the fellow-Scot who came and upstaged him as a missionary, and married his daughter to boot. It is unlikely that he resented this as indeed he had been the one to encourage Livingstone, a much younger man, to go north from the established stations and meet the natives on their own territory.

Moffat had been born at Ormiston in East Lothian in 1795. He began work as a gardener, but, like many of his fellow missionaries, he received the call when young and by 1816 had passed the scrutiny of the London Missionary Society and was at work in Namaqualand. In 1820, he settled in Lattakoo, the chief kraal of the Batlapin tribe in what became Bechuanaland, moving on when this was threatened to Griqua Town in 1824 and in 1825 to the base he made his own, Kuruman, on the edge of the Kalahari Desert. Here he worked hard healing, converting and, making full use of his training as a gardener, instructing the natives in agricultural techniques and irrigation.

He was a physically tough, no-nonsense missionary, completely dedicated to his calling. He translated the scriptures into Sechuana and in all his efforts received the full support of his wife, the daughter of his employer in East Lothian, whom he had married in 1819. She died after fifty years in Africa with him and in 1870 he returned to Britain, dying at Leigh in Kent, at the age of eighty-eight.

David Livingstone 1813-1873

—China's loss, Africa's gain

On 10 November 1871, John Rowlands, the product of a North Wales workhouse, met the son of a poor Scottish weaver in a remote and insignificant African village—and that single event

has been depicted on at least four postage stamps, the sort of treatment normally reserved for coronations or moonlandings. How did the two men get to that little village and why was the world agog to know about the meeting?

The Scot, David Livingstone, landed up in Africa for the paradoxical reason that he had his heart set on going to China. Born 13 March 1813 at Blantyre—a model working-class village in the west of Scotland's industrial belt—young David seemed to have his future planned out for him. The very street in which he was born was Shuttle Row and the shuttle was to be his master. From the age of ten, every morning at six o'clock, he left the 10-foot by 14-foot room that housed his entire family and made his way to the spinning mills. There he worked until eight at night repairing broken threads on the jenny.

Such a timetable was calculated to leave little time to ponder on alternative ways of life, but David Livingstone was not one to be hypnotised into a vegetable existence. He was an avid reader and fixed his book to the spinning jenny and "thus kept up a constant study, undisturbed by the roar of the machinery. To this part of my education, I owe my present power of completely abstracting my mind from surrounding noises so as to read and write with perfect comfort amidst the play of children or near the dancing and songs of savages."

By the time David was eighteen and a fully fledged spinner, he was spending his wages on lectures in medicine and divinity, two subjects that gripped his imagination. The choice was fortunate or perhaps inspired, for he eventually came to believe that he had to be a medical missionary. He attended lectures at Glasgow University, adding Greek and Chemistry to his old interests of Medicine and Divinity. The combination produced the very qualifications that the London Missionary Society were seeking and they accepted the large, gentle, gruff-looking man with his gauche manner and exceptional intelligence. David thought long about his calling and set his heart on China.

The Chinese were not, however, to be on the receiving end of

Livingstone's dedication. War broke out between Britain and China—and Africa was waiting in the wings to claim this qualified doctor and ordained minister for its own.

Livingstone travelled to Cape Town and, when waiting for the lumbering oxcarts to take him north to the frontiers of "civilised" Africa, set about learning Dutch and Sechuana. His first stop was Robert Moffat's mission at Kuruman. It was far too "established" for Livingstone, who felt that his fellow-Scot had nothing to offer him. He was to have second thoughts on that matter about a year or two later when he came and took Moffat's daughter Mary as his wife.

Livingstone saw his mission as that of a worker in amongst the natives. He travelled into the bush and got permission to set up a station there. This marked the beginning of a lifelong service to Africa, establishing himself in the eyes of the Africans as a selfless Christian doctor and servant—and in the eyes of Europe as a great, courageous explorer. He saw that the great disease of Africa—slavery—could be eliminated if only the country could be opened up to channels of real trade. In this context, exploration was an integral part of his task in the Dark Continent, even if lesser men cavilled at his travels and believed that they were made at the expense of his true calling to minister, heal and convert.

Taken as an explorer, his performance was immense. In 1849 he travelled to Lake Ngami, crossing the Kalahari. He travelled to the interior as far as the Upper Zambesi. On a two and a half-year trek, he became the first white man to witness the grandeur of the Victoria Falls. He returned to Britain in 1855, lecturing and publishing a book of his experiences. In 1858, he went back to Africa, this time as the British Consul at Quiliman. He led an expedition to Lake Nyasa, searched for the source of the Nile and then, as far as Europe and the world was concerned, disappeared. Those were the events that brought Livingstone to Ujiji late in 1872. But what was the Welshman doing there?

John Rowlands had emigrated to New Orleans at the age of

seventeen; seeking a new start in life. He was taken under the wing of a local merchant, Henry Morton Stanley, and in gratitude had assumed the name of his benefactor. The new H. M. Stanley fought in the American Civil War and afterwards established himself as a leading war correspondent in Europe. In 1869, he was summoned to a Marseilles hotel by James Gordon Bennett, son of the Banffshire Scot who had founded the *New York Herald*, and was given a simple instruction: "Find Livingstone." Bennett realised that to carry out such an order, Stanley would need a bottomless expense account. He got it.

Two years later Stanley was still searching, when he heard of a white man, such as he had described to many an African tribe over the past two years, tending to the sick in Ujiji.

Stanley's immortal "Dr Livingstone, I presume," introduced two men who had worlds to talk about, the old man with years of tales stored up, the young one with the news of the great outside world. The two even went on a short expedition together, the Scot riding on Stanley's donkey as depicted on a Burundi stamp. Stanley eventually left, unable to persuade Livingstone to return with him but carrying the news and notebooks of the great explorer.

Livingstone continued his work among the people he called savages but counted as brothers. In May 1873, he died at Chitambo village. His body was carried by faithful followers to the coast, a long and hazardous journey. In April 1874, the body was buried in Westminster Abbey.

BUILDERS OF NEW NATIONS

As Scotland in the eighteenth century slowly began to take some advantage of the union with her larger and more powerful neighbour, as trade expanded and the wealth of Scotland slowly developed with reform of land management, tree planting and the foundation and expansion of what are today the traditional industries of linen, whisky distilling and coal mining, one area of activity slowly closed as a career to the bright young men of the nation: politics. With Scottish politics in a stranglehold of the powerful factions, masterminded by a string of talented and ruthless managers, culminating in the Dundas "dynasty," there was little chance for a career in government or administration, which did not necessitate a move to London. A parallel restriction operated in the new industrial and agricultural developments: the wealth that was necessary to undertake these was invariably bound up with ownership of land and, increasingly, mineral rights.

The glittering prizes held out by the colonies where, the story went, any man with initiative and the will to work could get ahead, attracted the attention of very many of Scotland's most talented and assiduous citizens. Many thousands of them emigrated and found that the dreams were true—and, of course, an equally large number failed to make the grade and believed that the dreams were unattainable. One gets the impression, however, that the Scots tended to get more than their fair share of the first and less than their share of the second compared with the English, Welsh and Irish.

The Scots who feature in this section are clearly the cream of the cream and can in no way be taken as typical of the achievement of all Scottish emigrants. They can, however, be taken as representative of the drive and dynamism which many Scots took to their new homelands, in administration, development, politics and industry. It is worth remembering that this is not just a story of what the Scots did for these new colonies; it is also a story of what the freedom and opportunity and drive of the new colonies did for a large number of Scots who could never have achieved such satisfaction in the closed and claustrophobic society they had left. Look, for example, at the two Scots who went on to become Prime Ministers of Australia and the pair who did the same in Canada—and ask what these men could have reasonably been expected to achieve in their native land?

John Witherspoon 1723-1794 James Wilson 1742-1798

—they signed away Britain

When the great Declaration of Independence was signed on 4 July 1776, it was intended as an explanation to the American public, to Britain, to the world and to those who were to come afterwards just why the colonies had done what they did. In practice, the document became an inspiring, lucid announcement of the basic principles that lay behind the actions—principles that could apply to other nations and to other ages. The historic signing has been graphically painted by John Trumbull, and the signatories have been honoured on many postage stamps issued throughout the world to commemorate the United States' Bicentennial.

The signatories were, by the very nature of the struggle, of British extraction, with more than a fair share of them coming from the volatile Celtic fringe. Two of the signatories, John Witherspoon and James Wilson, were native Scots.

John Witherspoon 1723-1794

Hollywood could scarcely have improved upon the reality of the situation as the debate among the leaders of the American colonists built up to a climax, to the vote that would call for a complete break with Britain and to the signing of the Declaration of Independence. On 1 July 1776, the elements caught the spirit and mood of the occasion. Late in the afternoon, with the discussions well advanced but with some delegates still missing, a darkening summer storm engulfed the Pennsylvania State House in Philadelphia. A harsh shower rattled the windows and thunder rolled dramatically. Into the chamber burst the delegates for New Jersey, booted, spurred and rain-lashed. One of their number, John Witherspoon, President of the College of New Jersey, lost no time in joining the debate. No-one was in any doubt as to the vigour with which he would put his case or as to the side of the argument on which it would be thrown. Witherspoon was a hawk.

"The distinguished gentlemen from Massachusetts [John Adams] remarked as we came in that some colonies were ripe for independence. I would like to add that some colonies are rotten for the want of it!"

John Witherspoon had the distinction of being the only clergyman to sign the Declaration. While his signature was unique in that sense, it was certainly not unexpected. The fiery Witherspoon, head of one of the colonies' most important educational establishments, later to be known as Princeton College, had been a force in the politics of North America for some time, a hard-hitting figure, playing in some respects a rôle similar to that of the Reverend Ian Paisley in Northern Ireland in the 1970s.

Witherspoon had come to North America in 1768, with a reputation gained in the Church of Scotland as a staunch defender of the long-established practices against the new moves towards liberalisation. He saw clearly the world in black and white—and in true Knoxian tradition most of it was black, gloom and decadence in which his church had a duty to provide what hope and salvation there was.

He was born on 5 February 1723, to the Reverend James Witherspoon and his wife Ann Walker in the little village of Yester, East Lothian. He was educated at Haddington Grammar School and Edinburgh University and began his preaching in 1743, licensed by the Haddington Presbytery. He progressed to Beith in Ayrshire and then, in 1757, to the thriving comminity of Paisley. By this time he had married Elizabeth Montgomery and the couple had produced most of their ten children, only five of whom were to survive beyond infancy.

Over the next twenty years, Witherspoon established himself in the West of Scotland as a fervent bastion against any sell-out to the humanism of science and letters. His defence was long and bitter, with Witherspoon a master of satire and invective. When in 1768 he tired of the struggle in Scotland although he had been wooed by organisations in Rotterdam and Dublin, he decide to accept the post of President of the College of New Jersey.

He provided strong and welcome leadership to the Presbyterian Church in North America, preventing a split in the ranks and establishing a rapport with the Congregationalists. He was also a very able College president, building up the power and prestige of his institution and in particular laying the foundations for the concept of commonsense as opposed to intellectualism—a legacy which has never really left the US scene. It is difficult to imagine the Declaration of Independence being signed without the presence and approval of the dynamic Witherspoon.

He played an important administrative role in the colonists' struggle and in the building of the new nation. His last years were spent rebuilding his College. In old age he lost his sight, dying on 15 November 1794. He is buried in the President's lot at Princeton.

James Wilson 1742-1798

"Before we build the new house, why should we pull down the old one and expose ourselves to the inclemencies of the season? I speak for my constituents. If this Preamble passes, Pennsylvania will suffer an immediate dissolution of every kind of authority. The people will be instantly in a state of nature."

The contribution from John Witherspoon's fellow Scot, James Wilson, was, as the quotation above taken from an earlier debate suggests, that of a dove as far as separation from the British Crown was concerned. Wilson, twenty years younger than the fiery cleric, but strangely presented in the paintings and stamps which commemorate the signing of the Declaration as a white-haired Pickwickian figure with his distinctive steel-rimmed spectacles, was a quiet spoken intellectual, the colonies' acknowledged expert in constitutional law.

Born on 14 September 1742 to William Wilson and Alison Landale at Carskedo near St Andrews, he attended his local university and then went on to study at Edinburgh and Glasgow. He decided to seek his fortune in New York as a financial expert, but once there he turned to law. At first he practised on the frontier, a lawyer whose time was taken up mainly with land suits, but he soon returned to the more settled urban east and specialised in corporate matters. Business and politics were becoming inextricably mixed in the turbulent arguments of the British colonies and James Wilson, intellectually nimble, came to specialise in constitutional law, providing the colonies with one of its ablest academic protagonists in the argument with Britain.

He established that the London Parliament had no authority whatsoever over the colonies and was the first to spell out the philosophy that "all the different members of the British Empire are distinct states, independent of each other, but connected under the same sovereign".

This remained Wilson's position right up to the signing of the Declaration. He fought as hard and astutely to prevent the break with the British Crown as he had laboured to effect the break with the British Parliament.

His was, of course, the stance which did not win the day as far as the Crown was concerned, but he continued to play a valuable part in the new nation, developing the state constitution for Pennyslvania and, along with James Madison, playing a major part in establishing the relationship between federal and state rights and responsibilities which was at the heart of the structure of the United States of America.

Alongside his valuable constitutional role, he pursued a less attractive campaign for personal place, power and wealth. This lost him much of his popularity and at one time he was reduced to barricading his home against the public and militia in an episode dubbed the "Fort Wilson" affair.

He died in 1798 after an eventful career which earned him the epitaph in the American Dictionary of National Biography of "the prophet of nationalism and democracy".

William Paterson 1755-1810

—the gentle imperialist

"The weak Colonel Paterson thought more of botanical collection than of extending the cords of British sovereignty," sneered a critic of the gentle Lieutenant-Governor of Tasmania. It was a gibe which would not perhaps have wounded William Paterson and might even have pleased him.

He was born at Montrose on 17 August 1755 and, like many a Scot featured in this book, took the easiest road of all to emigration: the army. He joined the ranks as a youngster, with little of the belligerence associated with the profession. He was in fact a fervent and enquiring botanist. His posting to South Africa gave him an unrivalled chance to indulge his passion and between 1777 and 1779 he made a number of expeditions into Hottentot country, returning with his notebooks and specimen boxes brimming. He provided Britain with the first giraffe-skin it had ever seen.

After spending most of the 1780s on duty in India, he was appointed to recruit and command the New South Wales Corps for the defence and the control of the new convict colony at Botany Bay. This was no easy posting but Paterson was able to mount a number of scientific missions to the interior, plotting rivers, collecting plants. In 1804, he was appointed to look after Tasmania as Lieutenant-Governor. He held this post for six years, having to contend, as others had done more dramatically, with the difficult overlordship of the tyrannical Captain Bligh, Governor-General of New South Wales. Paterson was relieved of his post when Bligh was replaced by Lachlan Macquarie in 1810. He left for home on *HMS Dromedary*, but died on the voyage on 21 June 1810.

He left his botanical collection to the Natural History Museum in South Kensington and the soldier-administrator would surely have appreciated more than a triumphal arch the fact that a beautiful flower, *Lagunaria patersonii*, now bears his name and, on a more practical level, that the peach he introduced to New South Wales plays an important role in Australia's export wealth.

Lachlan Macquarie 1761-1824

—the Governor with compassion

A Scot was returning home. In the hold of his tubby ship were his big brown horse, Sultan, and his favourite cow, Fortune. For company, the two creatures had sheep, ducks, turkeys, geese, 106 fowls, seven pet kangaroos, five emus, seven black swans, Cape Barren geese, white cockatoos, bronzed-winged pigeons and parrots, all tended by some rather apprehensive Australian aborigines, tilting on the ocean for the first time. This was clearly no ordinary Scot.

Lachlan Macquarie, former Governor of New South Wales, had come to the end of his stint. He had taken up his post in 1809, replacing the autocratic and disgraced Captain Bligh and now, twelve years later, had completed a long and uniquely successful tour of duty.

The vital statistics of his rule were impressive enough. Fewer than 12,000 inhabitants had grown to almost 40,000, cattle had nearly increased tenfold, sheep had done so handsomely, while land under the plough had increased from 7,600 to 32,270 acres.

But Macquarie is remembered as much for character of the growth as for the tempo. He inherited the great convict colony, at the worst considered as one great open prison from which the inhabitants never escaped and in which their crimes would never be forgiven and certainly never forgotten. A barely less obnoxious view was that the colony provided a great opportunity to re-establish the untrammelled power of the landed gentry, with the benefits of slave labour from the convicts, a subject people in the aborigines and no danger from the liberalism and democracy that were undermining the upper classes at home.

Macquarie came to the colony with no preconceived notions that could be used to support either of these stances. Born in 1761 on the island of Ulva nestling in the jaws of big neighbour Mull, Lachlan Macquarie escaped the rigours and poverty of his inherited life by joining the army as a young boy. By the age of twenty-three he had spent nearly a third of his life in the barracks, including spells in North America and Jamaica. By 1788, he was in India and it was there that he had to spend most of his army career, with regular trips to get back to Ulva, a love and a link which he never lost.

By 1808, when the powers-that-be were on the look out for a military man to put an end to the naval colonial governors and in particular to "relieve" the blustering and ineffectual Captain Bligh in charge of the great penal colony of Botany Bay, the bluff, humane and experienced Lieutenant-Colonel Lachlan Macquarie, did not leap immediately to public attention. Indeed the Government appointed one Miles Nightingale to the post but he, deterred more by the low pay than by the dangers of the post, suffered an appalling attack of rheumatism in the right arm and wrist which made it impossible to carry out the writing associated with administrative duties and withdrew from the post. Macquarie, who had been delegated to accompany him with his 73rd Regiment (complaining that this was no way to be treated after twenty-five years in India with only two years' leave) was appointed to take over as Lieutenant-Governor of New South Wales.

Four days later Macquarie was presented to the King— during an audience at which Macquarie's old friend and doughty seaman, Lord Thomas Cochrane, who will figure prominently later in this book, was made a Knight of the Order of the Bath. On the next day, Macquarie discovered he had been promoted to a full Governor. Into the bustling, tense, penal colony came a man with great skills of leadership and administration and, more importantly for Australia, with a great humanity. His great dream was of a colony which would develop into something much more than a prison, into a dynamic thriving state, stimulated by encouragement and opportunity for those who came as convicts as well as those who came voluntarily to settle.

From the start the new Governor made it clear what his policy was to be. Once convicted men had served their term, he tried to clear forever the category of emancipist which in the colony he inherited meant a second-class citizen. He invited one-time convicts to his dinner tables, he opened the way for them to play a full part in the growth of a new exciting community experiment, he even reached the stage of appointing to the Bar men who had come to Australia under sentence themselves.

Such a policy won supporters rapidly from among the deprived classes; it won opponents no less readily from the privileged. Macquarie's twelve-year struggle was not an easy one, but it was one in which he had the fortifying support of Elizabeth, his charming and hard-working second wife.

Macquarie, originally given the promise of a pension if he would only stay at Botany Bay for eight years, added four more and when he retired from the post in 1821 was replaced by a fellow Scot, Sir Thomas Brisbane, a native of Largs who was to do more for Australian astronomy than for the welding together of the communities which had been pioneered by Macquarie.

As Macquarie left Sydney Harbour for the last time, young Robert Howe, the Continent's first native-born journalist, penned the report: "Australia saw her benefactor for the last time treading her once uncivilised, unsocial shores and *felt it to*. The parent and the child must endure the parting pang and Australia cannot repine at the varied events time brings about, for time has wrought cast and beneficial changes in her midst."

For all the purple prose, that passage reveals a real affection

D

and debt. Two years later, the colonists were mourning the death of the great man. His body was taken back to Mull and buried there—the tomb belongs to the National Trust for New South Wales and is under the care of its opposite number in Scotland. When Macquarie was born there was not a single European living permanently in Australia; at his death and due in no small part to his life, there was a thriving colony of communities where he had found a settlement of jailors and jailed.

John Alexander Macdonald 1815-1891 Alexander Campbell Mackenzie 1822-1892

—the architect and the builder

In 1873, Canada had its Pacific Scandal. Like the Marconi Scandal which was to muddy the waters of Westminster politics nearly forty years later, it concerned suspected misuse of Government access to information on large-scale communications contracts to feather personal or party nests. Both affairs, quickly in the headlines and just as quickly forgotten, performed political miracles; the Marconi Scandal managed to shut up Lloyd George for nearly two years; and the Pacific Scandal, with even more spectacular results, managed to prise from office, John Alexander Macdonald, leader of Canada, first Prime Minister of the first Dominion.

John Macdonald, born in Glasgow in 1815 and taken by his parents to Canada at the age of five, made spectacular use of the opportunities of the New World. He was appointed to the Bar in 1836, elected to the legislature of Canada West in 1844 and became a Queen's Counsel in 1846.

The law may have been his profession; politics were his calling. A talented dynamo of a man who could cajole, bully, ignore, hoodwink or lead fellow politicians, he was built for power. He flexed his political muscles in the legislature of his province as leader of the Conservative party and as premier. His vision went far beyond the boundaries of one province, however, and he saw a powerful federation of all the British elements in North America, united under the Crown and firmly resolved upon growth and order.

A man of strong opinions rather than strong principles, he was the right man to achieve that difficult dream. He hammered out a Great Coalition, espousing many political enemies in the cause of federation. When the Dominion was created there was no doubt as to who would be the first Prime Minister. Indeed, it seemed as if he had a divine right to the "throne" of Canada and he ruled, apart from that little hiccup of the Pacific Scandal, right up to his death in 1891.

It says a great deal for his resilience, following, and political skill that even after the set-back of loss of power, he swept through the subsequent elections of 1882, 1886 and 1891 with apparent ease. The Architect of Canada had to be an Autocrat; John Alexander Macdonald played the role with distinction.

The Architect's sweep of power from the founding of the Dominion onwards was interrupted in 1873 by a Builder, but a real and not a figurative one. Fellow Scot, Alexander Campbell Mackenzie, was a building contractor in Kingston, Ontario. Born at Logierait near Dunkeld in 1822, he was a self-educated stone mason who left Scotland in 1842 and set up his own business in Canada. By the time of the creation of the Dominion in 1867, he was a prominent Liberal politician, sitting in the Canadian Parliament.

When the Pacific Scandal broke and threatened the Conservative administration, the Liberals could hardly have chosen a more effective leader than the Builder. He was a man of transparent honesty, the very symbol of the public probity which the Pacific Scandal had so blatantly flouted. The Liberals swept to power and Macdonald was toppled.

Mackenzie, alas, was brimming with sincerity and devoid of vision. His administration, the first chance for the Liberal Party to show its mettle, was lacking in any real achievement and, indeed, it was not until the party acquired in French Canadian Wilfred Laurier a man with Macdonald's political gifts that it was able to make any impact on Canadian development.

Mackenzie led the Liberal Party until 1880 and died in 1892, within a year of the other Scot who had with Mackenzie monopolised political power in the first quarter of a century of the Dominion of Canada.

Andrew Fisher 1862-1928

George Houston Reid 1845-1918

—two Australian Prime Ministers

Andrew Fisher 1862-1928

In 1908, Australia acquired a new Prime Minister, Andrew Fisher and with him something of a record. Andrew Fisher had started life as a coal-miner in Ayrshire, Scotland and thus became the first really working-class leader of a Commonwealth country.

He was born in Kilmarnock on 29 August 1862 and as a boy followed the cruel but traditional trail to the local coal mine. By the age of eleven, he had broken away from his background and sailed to Queensland. He may have left the Ayrshire proletariat behind him, but he carried its political ideas with him.

He took an active part in state politics and in 1893 was elected to the Queensland parliament. He pioneered Labour politics at a time when the party was barely out of napkins in Britain and in 1904 he became a member of the first effective Labour administration in any of the British dominions.

He was to serve as Prime Minister in three administrations. In the 1910-1913 Government, he again made history by introducing the type of Labour legislation that would not hit other Commonwealth countries for decades: a land tax, maternity benefits, public welfare, and public works.

He built up the armed forces and had no hesitation in joining Britain's cause when the 1914-18 War broke out. He had worked under considerable stress and retired from politics in 1915, marking the end of Australia's Golden Age of Labour politics. He served as High Commissioner in London from 1916-1921 and died on 22 October 1928.

George Houston Reid 1845-1918

In 1916, the British House of Commons acquired a new Conservative MP who was different from any other. He was an ex-Australian Prime Minister. The pace of politics in the Dominion was obviously fast and furious if its politicians chose to retire to become Tory MPs at Westminster!

The man who achieved that unusual transition was George Houston Reid. He was born at Johnstone in Renfrewshire in 1845 and was only seven years old when his family emigrated to Melbourne. He was educated at the Academy in

Melbourne, later to be named Scotch College. He was called to the Bar in New South Wales in 1879 and was elected to the legislative assembly as the representative for East Sydney in 1880. He was Minister of Education in 1883 and premier in 1890. Reid was a leading advocate of the federation of the Australian states, and when this was achieved he was elected to the Commonwealth Parliament. He became Prime Minister of Australia in 1904, taking over from the short lived Labour régime. During his office he was a passionate promoter of free trade.

In 1909 he went the way of many of the Empire's Prime Ministers and moved to London as High Commissioner. It was a convenient spot from which to make his unusual move to the House of Commons.

Donald Alexander Smith 1820-1914

—driving in a spike at Craigellachie

In 1885, at the place in British Columbia, named after the village of Craigellachie on the Spey in north-east Scotland, a sixty-five-year-old gentleman, who was clearly wealthy enough not to have to indulge in such activity to earn a living, drove a metal spike into the ground and was cheered to the hilt. The Canadian Pacific Railway had been completed.

The man who had hammered in that final spike was Donald Alexander Smith and he more than any other man deserved the honour of striking the final blow for infrastructure! He had been the driving force behind the great Canadian Pacific Railway project, established as a chartered company in 1881 with the simple brief to complete the embryo railway and link Montreal with Vancouver, the Atlantic with the Pacific. The venture was to produce by 1900 a company controlling over 11,000 miles of track and owning not much less than twenty million acres of land.

Donald Alexander Smith was well prepared for the task. He had been born in Forres in 1820, twenty miles or so away from the original Craigellachie. Like many young Scots of his generation, he set off to win renown and reward with the Hudson Bay Company at the age of eighteen. He started as a clerk and thirty years later was the Company's top man in North America. His first hot potato was not, however, of the Company's making. In 1869, he was appointed special commissioner by the Dominion Government with his brief to go and sort out the serious uprising fomented by Louis Riel. Smith, with a combination of tact, discretion and toughness undermined the power of Riel and scotched the movement. The area, including the Red River with its tradition of Highland settlement, became part of Canada as Manitoba.

Smith's great passion was to link and to develop the territories of Canada. This and his track-record as an administrator made him a vigorous promoter of the Canadian Pacific Railway and led him to the honour of swinging that hammer at Craigellachie.

Smith was knighted by a grateful British Government in 1886, became High Commissioner of Canada in 1896 and Baron Strathcona and Mount Royal in 1897. He and his cousin Lord Mount Stephen had already carried through a number of large-scale philanthropic schemes including setting aside $1 million for a free hospital in Montreal to mark Queen Victoria's jubilee in 1887, topping up the fund with a further $800,000. In 1902, they did a repeat act across the Atlantic, settling King Edward's Hospital Fund in London with an endowment which produced £16,000 a year.

The outbreak of the Boer War led Lord Strathcona to mix philanthropy and patriotism, as he raised, paid and transported to South Africa, at his own expense, a regiment known as "Strathcona's Horse" recruited mainly in the North West Territories of Canada. Lord Strathcona died in London on 21 January 1914, at ninety-four—the oldest Scot to feature in this book.

George Brown
1818-1880

—power of the Press

Three isolated examples from his life might suggest that George Brown was a flop. As a politician, he was Premier of Upper Canada for just over a day. As a businessman, he came to Britain to try and sell Alexander Graham Bell's inventions—and forgot to show the one relating to the telephone. As a publishing tycoon, he was shot dead by a dismissed and disgruntled employee. The truth of his achievement was very different, for George Brown was a powerful and influential force in the development of modern Canada.

Born in Alloa, Clackmannanshire on 29 November 1818, George Brown moved with his parents to the USA at the age of nineteen. After half a dozen years or so running a Scottish Presbyterian newspaper, Peter Brown and his son George, out of sympathy with the anti-British republicanism of the USA settled in Canada and set up *The Banner* a publication supporting the Free Church.

George Brown moved from religious publications to a broader base and in 1844 launched the weekly *Toronto Globe*, Canada's first newspaper of any real influence, with a definite mission to reform political life. In less than a decade, *The Globe* became a daily, exercising considerable power in Upper

Canada, fighting successfully for a separation of Church and State, but failing against considerable Roman Catholic opposition from Lower Canada to get a similar secularisation of education.

George Brown played a powerful role with fellow Scot Alexander Mackenzie in building up Liberal politics in Upper Canada. He held a very strong belief in the need for a Confederation of all the British territories in North America. He was even prepared to sink his differences with the great Conservative politician of Canada, Sir John Macdonald, in order to bring about the unification of Canada as a member of the British Empire.

He turned down honours, including a knighthood, but when Liberal leader Mackenzie came to power, he accepted a seat in the Senate of the Canadian Parliament.

In 1880, a deranged former employee shot George Brown dead.

Sandford Fleming 1827-1915

—engineer with versatility

In 1977, Canada issued a stamp to commemorate the 150th anniversary of the birth of Sir Sandford Fleming, depicting the tall, handsome, gentle Scot in front of one of his many creations, a bridge on the Intercolonial Railway. The stamp was a particularly appropriate form of honour for Fleming, for although he was famous for his impressive engineering of canal and railway systems, in 1851 he designed his smallest creation—the three-penny beaver stamp that was Canada's first postage stamp.

Sandford Fleming was born in Kirkcaldy on 7 January 1827,

the son of Elizabeth and Andrew Greig Fleming. He was educated at the local school, and in 1845 he emigrated to Canada. He did his early engineering training on the Ontario Simcoe and Huron Railway and, along with other young and enthusiastic scientists and engineers set up the Canadian Institute. His early identification with his new nation is demonstrated by the fact that his postage stamp was designed after he had been in Canada for only six years.

Beginning with a wide range of projects including harbour development, he eventually specialised in railway surveying and engineering, working on the Intercolonial, the Canadian Pacific and the Newfoundland railways. He led the reconnaisance investigations through the prairies and the mountains to determine the most practical route for the Canadian Pacific. He displayed an uncanny sense of picking the right line and those of his recommendations which were turned down for political or other reasons were invariably taken up again at some stage.

Despite his rather mild manner, he displayed an immovable conviction in the correctness of some of his campaigns and became a figure of considerable importance on the Canadian scene.

He retired from his railway activities in 1880, but continued to devote his attention to communications on the grand scale. He was an indefatigable campaigner for links between the nations of the British Empire and urged and cajoled parties to co-operate in telecommunication links.

Allied with this activity was his campaign to get international acceptance of world-wide standard time. No doubt his experiences on the Canadian Pacific had led him to realise the problems of time zones across the broad span of Canada and to see just how important it was that the matter should be settled internationally. He was one of the most important participants at the International Conferences of 1888 and 1894 which set out to achieve such world-wide agreement.

Fleming became Chancellor of Queen's University at Kingston, in 1880 and occupied this post up to his death. He was knighted in 1897. He died on 22 July 1915, leaving among his achievements an impressive network of railways, an international agreement on time zones, a small volume of prayers which he used for his short religious services while working on the railway projects and that little stamp displaying the beaver.

Andrew Carnegie 1835-1919

—the Ruthless Cherub

In the summer of 1901, Andrew Carnegie arrived in Britain to find the newspapers carrying large advertisements placed by the makers of Mother Siegel's Syrup and announcing a competition: "How Mr Carnegie Should Get Rid of His Wealth." The prize, a gold sovereign, was to go to the reader or readers whose suggestion was accepted by Carnegie or happened to match his own ideas!

Rarely can an individual have been proferred so much advice on how the money he had extracted from society should be recycled. It was a subject on which Carnegie himself had already thought long and hard and there was no need for "Mother Siegel" to hand out any sovereigns despite the 45,000 suggestions they received.

Carnegie's strange and unique preoccupation with philanthropy stemmed from two competing forces acting upon him: democratic and even radical upbringing on the one hand

and unprecedented capitalistic success on the other. The former he owed to Scotland, the latter to the United States of America.

The radical input began early. Born in Dunfermline, ancient seat of the Scottish kings, Andrew Carnegie was the first child of William Carnegie and his wife, Margaret Morison. William was, in common with most of the workers in Dunfermline, a weaver, plying his hard, endangered trade in a small low cottage which served as home and factory. Margaret was the daughter of Tom Morison shoemaker and, more significantly for young Andrew, political activist, the vigorous and voluble protagonist of non-violent, radical reform. Andrew Carnegie's impressionable mind was exposed to the socialist doctrines of Dunfermline's skilled craftsmen and stimulated by the town's sense of history.

The development of power looms marked the twilight of the cottage hand-weavers and throughout the 1840s the pressures on Dunfermline's speciality of damask manufacture became more and more excruciating. William Carnegie lost his job. Margaret, running a shop by day and sewing shoes by night, bore the brunt of bringing up the family. The dreadful winter of 1847-1848 and the demoralising failure of the Great Charter on which Tom Morison and so many other radicals had pinned their hopes, brought the Carnegies to the point of decision: should they leave Scotland and try and earn a share in the prosperity of the New World? Margaret's younger sisters, Annie and Kitty, had married and made the move to Pennsylvania in 1840. The letters back home told of no easy El Dorado, but by the side of gloomy and depressed Dunfermline the opportunities of the USA were irresistible.

The Carnegies crossed the narrow neck of Scotland to the West Coast and set sail from Glasgow's Broomielaw. The quayside must have been busy, for in that year 188,233 people made the trip from Britain to North America. Andrew Carnegie relished the vivid, fresh experiences of the voyage and the long, crawling trip from New York to Pittsburgh via the

Erie Canal, and Lake Erie. Even pulsing Pittsburgh, which made Auld Reekie seem positively bucolic, enthralled the young lad.

The egalitarian, radical Scot was face-to-face with the booming New World and he pitched heart-and-soul into the business of making money. Starting modestly as a telegraph boy, he worked hard and earnestly to become a top telegraph boy. Promoted to a railroad boss's assistant, he became an indispensible railroad boss's assistant. In his chief's absence he displayed his formidable powers of organistion by taking charge of the potential disaster of a rail network failure and sorting out the problems calmly and smoothly. When a Mr Pullman came to his company to outline the advantages of a new-style sleeping compartment, Andrew Carnegie saw the potential, pushed the project and emerged with a financial share of the action.

To his enormous powers as a businessman, Carnegie added an early awareness of the power of investment. Barely eight years after arriving in USA, following a smallish investment of money raised within the family, Andrew Carnegie received from the Adams Express Company a cheque for ten dollars. He wrote later in life: "I remember that cheque as long as I live. It gave me the first penny of revenue from capital, something I had not worked for with the sweat of my brow, "Eureka," I cried, "here's the goose that lays the golden eggs."

Carnegie's career exploded, with his hard, aggressive and occasionally ruthless business tactics applied to oil, railway construction and financing, bridge-building, telegraphy, iron and steel. The child of Chartist Dunfermline became the daddy of Capitalist America, a tough shrewd, outgoing, cocky, idealistic cherub with a golden touch.

From his initial successes, Carnegie became aware of the responsibilities of such enormous wealth and settled down to a ding-dong haphazard league tussle with rival do-gooder Rockerfeller. But as he came closer to retirement and began to realise that it was just not possible to keep philanthropic pace with his capitalistic accumulations, he began to bring a controlled and directed approach to his charitable donations. The speed of giving remained unabated but the early patterns hardened and crystallised into a few special targets.

Dunfermline never lost its grip on Carnegie. "What Benares is to the Hindoo, Mecca to the Mohammedan, Jerusalem to the Christian. Dunfermline is to me." He went back often and purchased the estate of Pittencrieff, later to be given to the community which had cradled him, along with many other generous gifts. Scotland, too, benefited from its links with the millionaire, especially the universities, with large bequests aimed at paying for the fees of the students.

Another legacy from his grandfather Tom Morison, was a dedication to peace, and this again directed some of Carnegie's most lasting donations. He financed the building of the International Court of Justice at the Hague.

Church organs turned into another Carnegie specialisation, perhaps an example of how one simple donation could in the case of such a wealthy and impulsive giver grow into an almost unmanageable habit!

Perhaps the most lasting impact of Carnegie's giving came in his passion for learning, which he saw as the mark of the real gentleman, another legacy from Grandfather Tom. In the second half of the nineteenth century, free libraries were virtually unknown in the States and Carnegie was determined to change that. He gave libraries to Pittsburgh and Alleghany and then made an astonishing offer that he would donate a library building to anyone who was prepared to stock and maintain it.

At his death, he had established 2811 Carnegie libraries. Every state in the USA had at least one, Britain and Ireland had 660, Canada had 156, New Zealand had 23, South Africa had 13 and the British West Indies had 6, Australia had 4 and there was one in Singapore. Through the various trusts he had set up, his giving has continued, the most spectacular long-running philanthropy of all time.

John Muir
1838-1914

—father of the conservationists

In a log cabin in the wilds of Wisconsin, it is early morning, very early morning. A large home-made wooden clock ticks up to the set hour and triggers off an alarm mechanism. Slowly the cross-bar on which a bed is mounted tilts up and young John Muir is awake, vertical and ready to start his reading for the day. The mechanical device is John's answer to his father's pronouncement that he may read as much as he likes—but must not stay up late at night. Young John is an avid reader and in his quest, as one biographer put it, "to read every book he could buy exchange or borrow for miles around" the wooden wake-me-up, stand-me-up was the answer.

It was not the first time that the cold rigid discipline of his father had brought out the best in John Muir. He was born in Dunbar, on Scotland's east coast on 21 April 1833, first son and third child to Daniel Muir and Anne Gilrye. Schooling at Dunbar was supplemented by his father's daily demands— memorising sections of the Authorised Version, encouraged by a good helping of corporal punishment. Though it could have provided little consolation at the time, his grounding in the language of the Bible gave him a fine writing style for his later journals and bristling turn of phrase when he came to attack those who would despoil his beloved wildernesses.

In 1849, Daniel sailed off to the USA taking with him John, his sister Sarah, and his brother David. They established a homestead in Wisconsin and sent for the rest of the family.

Daniel's harshness in education extended to the young John's work. The boy, in his early teens, was given hard, sapping jobs that would have tested a mature man. No matter how strenuous the chores, John's zest for learning and reading never flagged. Thanks to his wooden device (he was proud of the fact that he was an ingenious whittler), he did enough reading to enter the University of Wisconsin, wandering through the courses, attracted to chemistry, geology and botany, but emerging without a degree.

He continued with his "ingenious whittling" and looked as though he might turn into an inventor, but in 1867 while working in a wagon factory, he suffered an injury to his eye which made close mechanical work impossible. By that time, he had started what was to become a life-long addiction: long tours on foot through the countryside. Not for him the brisk morning ramble, however. He set off on a walk from Indiana to the Gulf of Mexico, a thousand-mile hike, logged in a day-by-day journal, in which he discussed animals and plants, geological formations and forests, people and thoughts.

In California, he visited the Yosemite Valley and this was to be the focus of his studies for the next six years. His walks took him to Nevada and Utah, to the North-West and to Alaska—and as he went he filled some seventy books with sketches and observations. He married the daughter of a Polish immigrant Dr John Strentzel and bought from his father-in-law part of a fruit farm. From 1881 to 1891, he worked hard to establish this as a viable business, eventually providing enough money to look after himself, his wife and two daughters—and get back to his travels.

Two aspects of nature were especially riveting for John Muir: glaciers and forests. The first took him to Alaska and a glacier there bears his name; the second took him to the sequoia and pine forests of Australia and Africa. It was, however, his burning conviction that nature was something that had to be protected from the greed and thoughtlessness of man that won him a place in this book. In the latter part of his fruit-farm period—and before he started on his globe-trotting again—he was horrified to see the destruction of the Yosemite by sheep—"the hoofed locusts" was a phrase of his of which those Old Testament prophets would have been proud. His colourful, non-stop campaigning won over public opinion and a succession of Presidents and defeated the lobbying of the timber barons. Muir's advocacy of National Parks culminated in the conversion to his cause by Theodore Roosevelt.

The indefatigable Muir persuaded the politician to come camping with him, and in his first six years of office as President, Roosevelt established no fewer than sixteen new national parks, taking in 148,000,000 acres. In the battle "between landscape righteousness and the devil," the lean, magnetic charmer from Dunbar and Wisconsin had won. A stamp was issued by the USA in 1964, fifty years after his death as an acknowledgement of the lasting nature of that victory.

Leander Starr Jameson 1853-1917

—the Doctor who made it to the text-books

Lobengula, King of the Matabele, Protector of the Mashona, was in pain—and the emissary from Cecil Rhodes knew just what to do about it. Dr Leander Starr Jameson, known in South Africa simply as The Doctor, was able to relieve the agonies of the chieftain's gout speedily and simply, although the morphia treatment was, cynics have suggested, more to be commended politically than medically. (Coincidentally, Lobengula's father, Mzilikazi, had also suffered from painful gout, relieved by another Scottish visitor, the missionary Robert Moffat.) It certainly eased relations between the two men as effectively as it relieved the pain. The Doctor was made *induna* of a warrior regiment and invested with ostrich feather

E

headdress, oxtail and weaponry. It was the begining of a fertile connection for the ambitious Cecil Rhodes.

Rhodes had a vision of a British presence in Africa running from the Cape to Cairo. It was a vision he had been able to pass on to Dr Jameson when the two young men first met in Kimberley. Jameson was born in Edinburgh on 9 February 1853, to Robert Jameson, a Writer to the Signet in the city's legal profession, and Christina Pringle, daughter of a military Borders family. At the age of seven, he moved to London when his father decided to make a transition from the law to journalism. Robert Jameson died when Leander was still in his teens, but the young man had gone on to study medicine at University College London, graduating with distinction and being appointed as resident medical officer at the College's distinguished teaching hospital.

With a fine career in British medicine seeming certain, Jameson left London and went to work in Kimberley, the teeming diamond-mining centre of the world. The rough, pulsating, brash society of Kimberley was a world away from the London in which Jameson had studied, but The Doctor was fascinated by it—and by the mission of Rhodes to paint the Dark Continent red. The negotiations with Lobengula, to allow British interests to explore and prospect in Mashonaland were the first of many such tasks undertaken by Jameson in the furtherance of Rhodes' ambitions. The Doctor, confident, brash, charming and intelligent, pitched into his new life with enthusiasm, exploring, negotiating, probing. By 1891, he had given up his practice in the Cape and taken over the administration of Mashonaland, to provide settled government on behalf of the British South Africa Company. A bare two years later, the Matabele became the targets rather than the allies of the British, as a bloody war broke out in order to integrate forcibly the Matabele lands into Rhodes' burgeoning "empire." Lobengula was slain and yet another step was taken on the road to Cairo. Jameson visited London in 1895 and was hailed as a hero in the cause of colonialism.

On his return to Africa, Jameson began to lay the plans which were to convert him from bluff hero to incompetent scapegoat.

In the heart of the south of Africa lay the Transvaal. Established by Dutch Boer settlers moving northwards from Cape Colony, the Transvaal had been forcibly annexed by the British in 1877. The Boers had not borne this yoke for long and in 1880 rose up against the overlords, with military triumphs at Bronker's Spruit, Laing's Nek, Ingogo and Majuba. The British ceded complete self-government to the Boers under the suzerainty of Great Britain, this supervision being later restricted to foreign relations. In 1885, gold was discovered in the Transvaal's Witwatersrand and prospectors surged into the area. The military defeats of 1880 still rankled with the proud British and two new elements were added to the equation. The Transvaal was now a region of great potential wealth; and some of the incomers, the Uitlanders, including many British, were badly treated by the Boers. To the Rhodes "administration," the time was ripe for putting back the clock and bringing the Transvaal to heel.

An uprising was planned for 28 December 1895. Discontented Uitlanders would rise within the Transvaal, while Jameson would move in with company police stationed close to the border. The "spontaneous" uprising from Johannesburg never took place and Jameson, fretting on the doorstep of the Transvaal, decided to take positive action in the hope that this would spark off some action by the Uitlanders. He ordered the troops to march into the Transvaal under the command of Sir John Willoughby. The Boer commandoes followed relentlessly and inflicted heavy losses on the British before the soldiers surrendered.

Jameson to his credit made no attempt to pass the buck and took full responsibility for the invasion, which progressed into the text-books as the Jameson Raid. He was taken back to London and charged under the Foreign Enlistment Act. He was sentenced to fifteen months imprisonment and nearly died in Holloway Prison before he was released prematurely on the grounds of ill health. He returned to South Africa and made a distinguished contribution to politics and the development of the cause of federation. He and Rhodes remained staunch friends to the end, with Jameson taking over from Rhodes as leader of the Cape Progressive Party after his death in 1902. The Doctor was Prime Minister of the Cape from 1904-1908 and was knighted in 1909. He became president of the British South Africa Company in 1913 and died in England in 1917. His body was buried, alongside that of Cecil Rhodes, on the Matoppo Hills of Southern Rhodesia.

He perhaps unwittingly wrote his own epitaph when commenting on his sentence in London: "I know perfectly well that, as I have not succeeded, the natural thing has happened; but I also know that if I had succeeded, I should have been forgiven."

Catherine Spence 1825-1910

—the grand old woman of Australia

On 3 April 1910, Catherine Spence died in Australia, leaving in her will an estate worth £215. In financial terms it may have seemed that the young girl who left Scotland before she was fifteen, had not made full use of her remaining three score years and ten in the Land of Opportunity. But Catherine Spence's worth was not to be measured by money, and she was the only woman Scot who made it on to a postage stamp without the help of a prominent husband or even of a husband at all.

Catherine Spence was born near Melrose on 31 October 1825, the daughter of David Spence, lawyer and banker, and

Helen Brodie. The family were comfortably off and Catherine was sent to school at Edinburgh. In 1839, however, her father lost a lot of money in a speculation in wheat and Catherine had to be recalled from her Edinburgh nest. The family decided to seek for a change of fortune in Australia and David got off to a good start as the first Clerk to the first Adelaide Municipal Council.

Catherine was no less aggressive in carving out a career and chalked up an impressive list of firsts—the first woman to write an Australian novel, the first to promote the concept of kindergartens, the first woman political candidate. She began as a teacher and developed into a writer and then a journalist with a very special concern for social matters, concentrating on the plight of orphans, the need for government secondary schools for girls and on electoral reform.

A magnetic public speaker, she worked tirelessly to develop an international dimension to charity and was instrumental in setting up world-wide conferences to develop this theme.

Although she never married, Catherine Spence brought up three separate orphan families. When she died in 1910, she may have amassed only £215, but she had acquired the unique title of "The Grand Old Woman of Australia."

THE
HEALING
TOUCH

Near the end of the last century, a small boy, Philip Fildes lay dying in an elegant London home. For weeks, the infant was tended with care and skill by a Scot, Dr Murray, but eventually on Christmas Day 1871 the boy died. It was an incident no different from a thousand others, except for one key element: the boy's father was the distinguished Victorian painter Luke Fildes. For nearly a dozen years, the image of the caring doctor and the dying child haunted Fildes and eventually he came to produce a painting to try and recapture the atmosphere of that death scene. The painting, simply entitled "The Doctor," was a tribute to the dedication of that one physician and through him to the profession. It was an instant success, drawing visitors to the gallery, stimulating reproductions not only in Britain but also in the States where Ansteys produced a pirated engraving which reputedly sold a million copies.

A leading member of the medical profession addressing students about to graduate paid this tribute to the work: "A library of books written in your honour would not do what this picture has done and will do for the medical profession, in making the hearts of our fellow men warm to us with confidence and affection. Above everything, whatever may be the rank in your profession which you attain, remember always to hold before you the ideal figure of Luke Fildes' picture and be at once gentle men and gentle doctors."

The painting has been reproduced three times on stamps, notably in an early US commemorative to honour the medical profession. It is particularly appropriate that the doctor inspiring the painting was a Scot and to all intents an unknown one at that: he can serve to stand not only for the profession but also for the contribution made by Scots in the nineteenth century.

At the beginning of the seventeenth century, Scotland had no tradition in medicine. A century later the Scots were a common sight in the great European medical centre of Leyden. A century later than that in 1800 Edinburgh was poised to become the medical centre of the world. Between 1800 and 1850, Scotland produced nearly 8000 out of Britain's 8291 graduate medical practitioners and the Scottish doctor became as well recognised an international character as the Scottish soldier and the Scottish engineer were becoming.

It is against this background of the Scottish medical tradition, which as you will see from this book produced not just doctors but also explorers, administrators, soldiers and writers, that the three Scottish individuals who have been singled out for postage stamp prominence should be seen. They are here because they produced the vital breakthrough in the fight against three of man's most telling foes: tuberculosis, malaria and infection.

Robert Philip
1857-1939

—'the man that fights tuberculosis'

The young assistant was uneasy. He did not have a patient on whom the doctor could demonstrate to the students the way in which they should study the suspected tuberculosis sufferer. He hurried out into the Edinburgh street, picked upon a suitably undernourished lad and after some haggling over a suitable bribe took the boy back to the surgery. It turned out to be a "lucky" choice. The Doctor described the "transparent luminosity of the skin, the dry hair and the listless attitude" of the patient, early signs of the active tubercule—and admitted him as suffering from meningeal tuberculosis.

The fact that nowadays, a short half-century after that incident, it would be very difficult indeed to pop out into the streets of any British or foreign city and pluck out a TB sufferer can be credited more to that doctor, Sir Robert Philip, than to any other man.

Born on 29 December 1857, son of a Glasgow minister, Robert Philip was educated at Edinburgh High School and then at the capital's university. After a first degree in the arts, he progressed to medicine, with spectacular academic success. His brilliance was unmistakeable; the field to which this brilliance was to be applied was decided during his postgraduate work on the Continent. In Vienna, he encountered for the first time the newly discovered tubercule. In Berlin, he sat at the feet of the man who had discovered it, Professor Robert Koch.

Philip returned to Edinburgh, his mission clear: to apply the discovery of Koch to the realities of urban tuberculosis. His Professor was less than enthusiastic; established thought was relinquishing slowly the belief that the consumption that laid waste operatic heroines and the phthisis which is familiar an entry in the death certificates of the nineteenth century were hereditary diseases. He tried to discourage the enthusiastic crusader: "Don't think of such a thing. Phthisis is worn to a thin thread. The subject is exhausted."

Philip was not one to be put off lightly. In 1887 he received a Gold Medal for his work on the aetiology of phthisis, the causes of the wasting away of the lungs that occupied in the minds of his contemporaries, medical and lay, the place reserved today for cancer. His great contribution to medicine was not, however, to be an academic one. In the same year that he cherished that Gold Medal, he also took charge of the Victoria Dispensary for Consumption and Diseases of the Chest, the world's first centre established to mount an organised attack on tuberculosis. Starting in a two-room flat at 13 Bank Street, just off Edinburgh's teeming Royal Mile, the project expanded to Lauriston Place and then to Spittal Street, becoming in 1894 the Royal Victoria Hospital.

Philip had set off on a long, honourable and successful battle against a disease that awed his fellow doctors. One Egyptian doctor, trained by Philip, recounted in later years the sense of wonder he felt when first meeting "the man that fights tuberculosis." The hallmark of Philip's work was the comprehensive, total approach he took to the task. The pattern was established early—the so-called Edinburgh System that was to be exported throughout the globe. It consisted of a dispensary, sanatorium, farm colony, open-air school and hospital for the advanced cases. It emphasised the need to go into the "tubercular nest," the home or household from which each case sprang, to track down the contacts, "the march past" in Philip's phrase.

Philip combined a wholehearted approach, remarkable teaching skill and the welcoming of new additions to his armoury. The formula attracted disciples by the score, many from overseas, trained and sent back to spread the Philip Gospel, the good news of the Edinburgh System.

Philip accumulated honours, distinctions and responsibilities as speedily as he gathered disciples—knighted in 1913, President of the Royal College of Physicians in 1917 (a post he held for five years, a feat that had not been achieved for 160 years), Professor of Tuberculosis at Edinburgh in the same year (the first such chair in the British Empire). His honours from overseas countries were no less impressive. And all the time he developed and intensified his attack on the disease, with undeniable success. He told the Milbank Foundation in the USA in 1910 that if it pursued his methods it could produce a 40 per cent drop in mortality in ten years. By 1920, that was almost exactly the improvement which had been achieved.

He was a talented, relentless worker, brilliant administrator and a convinced crusader. Hardly any element in the conquest of TB did not benefit from his involvement, from the National

Association for the Prevention of Tuberculosis founded in 1898 to establishment of a herd of tubercular-testing cattle at Gracemount, south of Edinburgh, from BCG—a drug advocated by Philip sixteen years before Britain got around to accepting it—to the campaign to make TB a notifiable disease. Philip's attitude was summed up in a passage from a speech he gave in 1912 to the International Congress on Tuberculosis in Rome: "Tuberculosis has accompanied civilisation. Mankind is responsible for tuberculosis. What an ignorant civilisation has introduced, an educated civilisation can remove."

Sir Robert Philip died in 1939, the last of the great Edwardian physicians, global crusader and evangelist. On the centenary of his birth, Belgium commemorated him on a stamp, while the National Association for the Prevention of Tuberculosis placed a plaque on a wall of the city where he worked but which has to a large extent neglected him. It reads: "Near this place in 1887, Dr Robert W. Philip founded a tuberculosis dispensary, the first clinic in the world dedicated to fighting a disease of which he foretold Man's eventual mastery. That vision has brought hope to many lands."

Ronald Ross 1857-1932

—putting the finger on the fly

Ronald Ross knew more about mosquitoes than any other person in the world. They had been the object of his almost neurotic attention for five years and on a hot August day in 1897 he was getting to know a new type. He had caught, killed, dissected, studied, logged and noted *ad nauseam* the common grey and brindled types but now the Indian boys had brought into his Calcutta laboratory a new "dapple-winged" type.

Ross fed the ten flies on the blood of a brave volunteer, the malaria-troubled Husein Khan, and the investigation began in earnest.

Ross killed and dissected two of the mosquitoes; nothing unusual. By the following day, two had died. Fearing that he might lose his stock before he had had a chance to study them, Ross killed and dissected a further two; still nothing. He was now left with just four of what scientists were eventually to call anopheles mosquitoes. On the morning of 20 August, he found that one of these had died. He ate a hurried breakfast at the Army Mess and returned to the laboratory to dissect the dead fly; nothing.

He was now left with just two mosquitoes and he set to work. The first of these provided Ross with his Eureka. In the stomach wall of the first insect, he noticed under the microscope some tiny specks of black or dark-brown pigment. Were these the same as those traces that had been noted in the blood of malaria victims by Alphonse Laveran nearly twenty years earlier? Ross was convinced that they were, and that he had found at last the link between the disease and the fly, the first step towards curing one of man's most long-standing scourges. For Ross—and later for the world—20 August 1897 was Mosquito Day.

Ronald Ross, the "Dragon Slayer" as one of his biographers was to call him, had plenty of good excuses for *not* becoming a great scientist. Born at Almora, a station in the foothills of the Himalayas, the first of ten children of a distinguished Scottish Army Officer, Ross received an education which was desultory in the extreme, consisting of a dame's school followed by some far from top-flight English boarding schools. His own leanings towards art and poetry, music and drama, were countermanded by a stern Victorian father who wanted to see his son follow him into service in India. The stresses of these two conflicting influences never really left Ronald Ross, but as a dutiful son he entered St Bartholomews Hospital in London and looked set for an undistinguished medical career. He squeezed through the first part of the examinations and failed at the final hurdle. He did a few voyages as a ship's surgeon, a branch of medical practice where entry qualifications were not unduly stringent. He eventually completed his medical examinations and joined the Indian Medical Service serving as an Army officer in Madras, Burma and the Andamans. As the responsibilities were light and the work undemanding, he was able to pursue his artistic inclinations, reading, writing poetry and prose and learning Italian, French and German.

At that stage, all the signs suggested that this scion of a talented family, descended on his father's side from the Rosses of Balnagowan, was to sink into a comfortable obscurity. But the mixed-up Ronald Ross was in search of a mission. "I was neglecting my duty in the medical profession. I was doing my current work, it was true, but what had I attempted towards bettering mankind by trying to discover the causes of those diseases which are perhaps mankind's chief enemies?" This was written later, after his great discovery, but there is no reason to doubt that it throws some light on the state of mind of the young Ross in his Indian days.

In 1888, he came back to Britain on leave and instead of spending this on rest and recreation (which he did not entirely neglect, as he did at least return with a bride), the young doctor acquired the newly introduced Diploma of Public Health, studied bacteriology under Emanuel Klein and got hooked on the wonders of microscopy. On his return to India, he became interested in research and in malaria, but it was not until he returned to Britain on leave in 1894 that his targets were clarified.

He met the great Aberdeen scientist Patrick "Malaria" Manson, son of the Laird of Fingask, who set down for him with convincing evidence two basic starting points: one, Alphonse Laveran had discovered in 1880 parasites in the blood of malaria victims; two, mosquitoes might in some way play a part in the transmission of these.

Manson supporters have claimed that he handed Ross the

solution on a plate—although Manson himself was never in any doubt as to the immense contribution made by Ross. What he did do was show Ross what he was looking for—those dark-brown parasitic flecks—and suggest where he might look—in mosquitoes.

Ronald Ross returned to India, fired with resolve. The task was enormous. He had not been trained in research and he was cut off from help, advice and encouragement, as the Indian Medical Service had no tradition of research work. His superiors were less than sympathetic to someone wanting to go off and peer through a microscope at flies. Malaria sufferers were understandably reluctant to come along and offer themselves and their blood to this strange doctor. Perhaps most important of all, Ross was entering a completely uncharted field. "Mosquitoes are mosquitoes" would perhaps sum up the world's knowledge of the creatures at that time. Ross would have to subject the flies to intense and structured investigation and classification—and would have to do the same with the parasites, where there was an even greater variety to contend with.

The genius of Ross—for the genius was undoubtedly there—lay in his burning conviction in the value of his quest and the correctness of his field of study. Many thousands of miles away, Manson continued to support him by letter.

Five years and countless mosquitoes after Manson had suggested the question, Ross came up with the answer in those flecks of dark brown lurking in the stomach wall. Having made the great discovery of the parasite that is present in both malaria-victims and mosquitoes, Ross had to trace the life-cycle of that parasite. The handicaps that had slowed down his search did not disappear. Regimental duties prevented him from carrying out work on humans; he was forced to use cage-birds and came up with a life-cycle he suggested might apply to humans.

Appropriately, the first announcement of Ross's discovery of the life-cycle was given on 28 July 1898 by Patrick Manson to a meeting of the British Medical Association being held in Edinburgh.

The validity of the work done on cage-birds to the human malaria situation was speedily confirmed, by a team headed by Battista Grassi working in the malaria areas of Italy. The Italians claimed credit for the discovery—ironically it was the Italian language that had, in the name "malaria" (bad air) perpetuated the misconception that attributed malaria to the miasma of swamps and marshes.

In 1902, the Nobel committee, meeting to award the second round of what were to become the most prestigious honours in science, named Ronald Ross as the man to receive the Prize for medicine and put the issue beyond any doubt.

Ross had no illusions about the struggle ahead. The discovery of the life-cycle of the malaria parasite had not ended his quest; it had merely changed the direction. He left India in 1899 and began the second stage of his battle against the "Dragon." He lectured at the new School of Tropical Medicine in London, he became Professor of Tropical Medicine in Liverpool, returned to London's King's College, teaching, cajoling, urging public health programmes, carrying out work in malarial areas of the world. In 1926, he became head of the Ross Institute of Tropical Hygiene and it was there that he died in 1931.

A pugnacious, erratic critic of anyone he saw as standing in the way of the defeat of malaria, Ross was an abrasive, controversial man in many ways. Although in this aspect differing from Robert Philip, the malaria-fighter making enemies and opponents as quickly as the tuberculosis-fighter made friends and disciples, the two men had much in common. Born in the same year, both started from the valuable but purely theoretical hint offered by others (Laveran and Koch) and devoted themselves single-mindedly to one disease, seeking its causes, investigating the means by which it was spread and then campaigning with passion for the total armoury of weapons to eradicate it.

In May 1857, two events happened in India—the outbreak of the Indian Mutiny and the birth of a son to a proud Scottish soldier on the frontiers of Empire. The history books, in concentrating on the first, may not have got it right after all.

Alexander Fleming 1881-1955

—the battle against infection

The Fleming boys had gone to London in search of jobs. They had rented a house in the Marylebone Road and, well cared for by their sister, Mary, were doing quite well.

They had come to the capital well prepared. Born and reared on a 800-acre hill farm of Lockfield in Aryshire, they had grown up taking full advantage of all the physical bonuses of an open-air country life, while their father, Hugh, had made sure their schooling had not been neglected, rounding off a spell at the local village school with a couple of years at Kilmarnock Academy.

The youngest of the boys was Alexander. Born 16 August 1881, he was the son of his father's second marriage, entered into when Hugh was sixty years old. Alexander had found a job in London as a clerk with a shipping firm. Then he came into a small legacy. It must have been a tempting windfall for a young man in the great metropolis. The canniness of the Scot, helped by the admonitions of the older brothers, persuaded Alexander to use the money to get some education.

He worked hard and set his sights on getting into St Mary's Hospital. Long hours and application took him to within reach of that goal. Luck again came to the young man's aid. St Mary's had on its staff Sir Almoth Wright, the greatest authority on vaccine therapy. It also wanted young Alexander

F

Fleming, not because it had spotted some hidden genius or detected a brilliant research scientist, but because it badly needed his talent, acquired from hours of boyhood rabbit-shooting, in the College Rifle Team!

Alexander Fleming caught up quickly for a late-starter and in 1908 he passed his finals with more than a little to spare, being awarded the Gold Medal at the University of London. His thesis was on the subject of acute bacterial infections.

World War I gave Fleming a traumatic introduction to the very real horrors of infection. He served as a captain in the Army Medical Corps and was mentioned in despatches. Into his centre at Boulogne came a never-ending stream of casualties. Bacteria were wreaking havoc with the wounded and antiseptics were useless, doing more damage to the living tissue than to the rampant bacteria. The experience clarified Fleming's resolve. He was to seek out an antibacterial substance that would not attack the living tissues of the body.

This work was undertaken alongside the teaching of bacteriology at St Mary's, with Fleming being appointed Hunterian Professor in 1919 and Arris Gale lecturer at the Royal College of Surgeons in 1928. In 1921, Fleming discovered a substance which he called lysozyme, to be found in tears and in certain parts of the body. This was not the answer but it encouraged Fleming to press on with his quest. It was a long quest.

Then in 1929, luck played its part in Fleming's life again, with "a triumph of accident and observation." Fleming was concentrating on influenza germs and had cultivated a number of bacteria colonies of staphylococci on plates within his laboratory. Fleming, it was later held, was a little remiss as far as his cleaning up of plates and dishes was concerned. Today, he would have been locked away in a dust free, germ-free, luck-free plastic-coated room. In 1929, such laboratories were less common and a speck of mould floated through the open window of Fleming's laboratory to settle on one of his plates of well-nourished bacteria.

Fleming first noticed its presence by the effect it had had on the bacteria. The mould which developed on the plate created a bacteria-free zone around itself, killing off the neighbouring staphylococci. Hunch and training led Fleming to separate the mould into two portions and put these away for investigation. When he came to look at the mould and what it could do, the results were startling. The liquid mould culture consumed the bacteria put before it with spectacular consistency. Fleming drank half a glassful. It did not harm him. He started diluting the culture and found that even down to one part in 800 it could destroy bacteria. The combination of death to bacteria, life to human tissue did exist. Eventually scientists were to work out just how this selective killing took place—the mould attacked cell walls, which plants and bacteria possess, but which animals do not.

Eventually Fleming identified the spore and named it *penicillium notatum*. He had found his wonder substance. He told the world about it in the *Journal of Experimental Pathology* in 1929. The story was far from finished. A dozen years later, Fleming's discovery interested the talented Australian Howard Florey who headed an Oxford research team and to him fell the task of making it a reality as far as medical treatment was concerned. Fleming never claimed any royalties or financial cut from the development of penicillin and the race to convert discovery into production was pursued on both sides of the Atlantic.

In 1944 bacteriologist Alexander Fleming was knighted and in 1945 he shared with pathologist Florey and biochemist Boris Chain the Nobel Prize for the teamwork which went in to giving the world penicillin. He died in London in 1955.

INVENTORS &
DISCOVERERS

Serendipity—the happy talent for discovering things—derives its name from an old word for Sri Lanka. It would be more appropriate if it had taken the form "Caledonity," for surely no nation has notched up quite so many discoveries and inventions as Scotland. Something in the nature of the Scots produces a quest for improving, simplifying or perhaps merely making more profitable the many and varied day-to-day activities.

Scottish inventions have been logged and listed almost *ad nauseam* but it is perhaps worth reminding readers that such household names as Dunlop and Mackintosh, derive from Scottish inventors, that the men who gave their names to Lee-Enfield rifles or Buick cars were Scots, that the bicycle and the vacuum flask, the kaleidoscope and the television set, radar and even appropriately enough in the context of this book, the adhesive postage stamp all originated from this ragged northern end of an offshore island to the west of the great Euro-Asian landmass.

The products of the inventive Scottish mind feature on hundreds of postage stamps; in this section, the inventors and discoverers featured are those who have been specifically singled out for a commemorative honour.

John Napier
1550-1617

—mathematics' greatest magician

On 28 July 1619, Johannes Kepler, one of the founding fathers of modern astronomy, wrote a letter to the Laird of the estate of Merchiston, on the south-west edge of Edinburgh. The letter is fascinating for three distinct reasons.

Firstly, it emphasises the astonishing contribution made not only to mathematics but also to such sciences as astronomy and navigation by the tables of logarithms invented, compiled and published by John Napier of Merchiston. Secondly, the amazing fact emerges from the letter that Kepler, one of the most perceptive mathematical minds in Europe and the most ardent user and promoter of the "magic numbers" that had made possible the fluent handling of the large and complex numbers encountered in astronomy, had no idea whatsoever of how Napier had arrived at the tables. He was in fact writing to ask Napier to publish the secret of his invention. Thirdly, the letter was written nearly twenty-eight months after Napier's death, a telling reminder of just how far from the mainstream of European thought Scotland had become in that century of vicious feuds and political turmoil, temporarily suspending the traditional links of trade and scholarship with the Continent.

Just what was it that Napier had produced to put Kepler and generations of scientists and mathematicians in his debt? The answer to that question is not difficult—although to explain *how* he produced his tables is another matter.

Think about your own mathematical experience. No matter what level you have now achieved, you will certainly have realised at a very early stage that the basic juggling with numbers comes in a variety of stages of difficulty. At the bottom of the league, simplicity itself, come the operations of addition and subtraction. Moving up a league in difficulty, you come to multiplication and division, much more complex operations, especially where large numbers are involved. But you are not finished there: move up to the next league and you come to powers and roots, impregnable to mental processes and pretty resistent to pencil and paper.

For centuries these "leagues" of difficulty were accepted as an unalterable part of the nature of mathematics. Then in 1614, John Napier, hitherto best known to the reading public as a writer of lengthy and learned attacks on Papal religion, produced a book dedicated to Prince (later King) Charles. The book contained mysterious tables of numbers and instructions on how to use them. In essence, they produced the most devasting step to simplify mathematics that had ever been taken. Multiplication and division became, using the magic numbers, a matter of addition and subtraction; and powers and roots also dropped down a league, becoming merely multiplication and division. And as if this were not enough, the Napier system treated complex and large numbers just as if they were simple and small. To find the fifth root of 23,298 was no more difficult than finding the square root of 14.

If the great Kepler could not understand how the tables of what Napier called logarithms were compiled—but had no doubts about what they meant in terms of simplified mathematics, lesser mortals could hardly be blamed for believing that these were magical, produced not by genius and application but by revelation or incantation. The "magician" who produced them had been born in Merchiston Castle in 1550, his father still under sixteen years of age. He was educated at St Andrew's University and later probably at Paris. He returned to Scotland in 1571 and in the following year married Margaret Stirling. He settled down to the sort of life expected of one of his class, managing his estate, involving himself in the convoluted and ruthless politics of the age, fathering thirteen children, haggling over inheritances, at one stage fixing the prices of shoes and boots in Edinburgh twice a year.

But Napier was much much more than a typical landowner. He had inherited a restless and probing mind. No matter what he was involved with, he was determined to put that fertile brain to work on it. Indeed at one stage he was accustomed to sending a message across the stream to the owner of the lint mill at Edrick asking him to turn off the mill as it was disturbing his train of thought. As a manager of an estate, he was a leading explorer of the possibilities of fertilising.

He invented a hydraulic screw and revolving axle to pump water out of coal-mines. But in those days the arts of peace were less important than the arts of war, and Napier produced designs for mirrors to set fire to the enemy sails in the event of invasion and a "chariot of metal, double-musket proof, the motion of which was controlled by those within and from which shot was discharged through small holes." Also in keeping with the argumentative and intolerant spirit of the times, he was a leading theological debater, producing voluminous contributions to the Protestant attack on things Papal.

But for all these notable contributions to husbandry, religion and warfare, it was really from his enduring hobby of mathematics that Napier's fame derives. Here as elsewhere in his thinking, his prime aim was efficiency. He was out not to expand the realms of mathematics but to make administration of the existing realm easier and more efficient. The methods he found were ingenious, finger-length rods used as a calculator, a mechanical computer, but most of all the imaginative concept of artificial as opposed to real numbers. This led him to the tables of logarithms, reducing all numbers to a power of a base number. In the course of these probings, incidentally, Napier also managed to invent the decimal point and the whole concept of decimal numbers.

Perhaps it was symbolic of Napier's essentially practical mind that he should publish the tables before he published the work on how they were made up. He died at Merchiston Castle in 1617 and never got the letter from Kepler, but his explanation of his "magic" was published just after his death.

When, more than 350 years later, Nicaragua came to produce a rather grandiosely titled series of stamps of scientific formulae, "The Ten Mathematical Equations that changed the face of the Earth," it was only fitting that Napier's contribution should feature, alongside symbols of navigation and astronomy. It is also worth noting that a gap of around 1700 years existed between Archimedes and the next great mathematician chronologically speaking—John Napier, Laird of Merchiston Castle.

Alexander Graham Bell 1847-1922

—teacher of the deaf, inventor of the telephone

Dom Pedro II, Emperor of Brazil, owed his title in no small part to the Marquess of Maranhao, a Scottish inventor better known for his naval exploits and by his earlier title of Lord Thomas Cochrane. In 1876, Dom Pedro was to repay that debt in a small way to another, more famous inventing countryman of Cochrane's. The Emperor was visiting the great Centennial Exhibition held in Philadelphia to celebrate one hundred years of US independence—and the show was going, as they say, like a fair. One stand, however, was not receiving a great deal of attention, but Dom Pedro recognised the man standing there as Alexander Graham Bell, the great expert in speech training and elocution and particularly in the training of the deaf. The Emperor had attended one of the Bell's speech training sessions at the University of Boston and, attracted to a familiar face, went over to talk to him. Bell, anxious to get so famous a personality to look at, or rather listen to, his new invention, asked him to put his ear to the apparatus being displayed. Tentatively the Emperor did so, and then dropped the instrument, exclaiming, "Great Heavens! The thing talks!" Bell's telephone became the lasting hit of the show and Bell, the most honoured Scot of all time as far as postage stamps are concerned.

There were two distinct pathways leading to the invention that was to sweep the United States. The first starts with a poor German physics teacher, the second with a Scottish teacher of the deaf.

Phillipp Reis in 1860, in his own words, "succeeded in inventing an apparatus that enables me to convert audible sounds into visible signs and with which moreover sounds of every sort may be reproduced by the galvanic current at any distance. I called it the Telephone." Despite Reis' many efforts to "sell" the idea to the men of science, he never succeeded and a few years later the invention had been relegated to the columns of a German magazine under the heading "A Toy for Clever Boys." At the age of forty, Reis died, declaring in his last years, "I have given a great invention to the world, but I must leave it to others to develop it."

History shows that the task of converting Reis' screeching needle into a means of conveying speech over distances passed to a talented and persistent Scot, who despite his successes, was always to describe himself not as an inventor but as "a teacher of the deaf."

Alexander Bell (the name Graham was acquired at a later stage) was born on 3 March 1847 in a flat just off Edinburgh's elegant Charlotte Square. Like many of the Scots featured in this book, he was born into something of a family specialisation; unlike most of those, he became part of it rather than rejected it.

The Bells were basically elocutionists. Alexander's grandfather and father passed on to him the gift of a fine rich voice and musical ear—and a flair for teaching speech not just to the shy and stammering but also to the deaf. Another no less important legacy was the environment of nineteenth century Edinburgh in which curiosity and experiment were encouraged almost above all other virtues. Alexander's early experiments were for the most part connected with the plants and creatures around the cottage in Trinity, a few miles to the north of city centre, where the Bells spent much of their holiday time. A notable exception was Alexander's first mechanical invention which was undertaken to help a neighbouring miller at the Water of Leith to clean the husks off his wheat.

At the age of fifteen, Alexander went to London where his

grandfather Melville was working. The old man, accounted by many to be better than Dickens at reciting Dickens, was to teach young Alexander the rudiments of elocution and declamation. His grandson was also introduced to the comparative sophistication of the big city and, significantly for future developments, to the great English scientist Sir Charles Wheatstone, who showed him a speaking machine designed to reproduce the sound of the human voice. Alexander was soon ready for a job and returned to Scotland, to the shores of the Moray Firth where he was a pupil-teacher of music and elocution in Elgin. He then taught in Edinburgh for a brief spell at the famous Donaldson's School for the Deaf until, troubled by bronchial illness, he decided to go off to the United States to see if a change of air would improve his health. At Boston, he specialised in the teaching of deaf mutes.

By upbringing and tradition, he was never a man to confine his energies to conventional boundaries and he probed any avenue which involved study or understanding of the human voice and the mechanisms of producing it and hearing it.

Like his father, he married a deaf woman much younger than himself. In addition to considerable understanding and companionship, the match brought Bell a small amount of money from his wealthy father-in-law with which he could indulge his experimentation. Along with a mechanic Tom Watson, he spent a great deal of time experimenting with sound and electricity. His expert ear detected that when transmitting musical notes he was also succeeding in transmitting the harmonics which characterise speech. He realised that there was a possibility of transmitting speech.

In March 1876, the moment of truth in the experiments came when he spoke to his assistant in the next room, "Mr Watson come here—I want you." In time for the great Centennial Exhibition he had produced his telephone. It was based on a metal diaphragm suspended close to coils wound on magnetisable iron cores. When sound waves struck the diaphragm, they created changes in the magnetic field and hence changes in the electric current. At the other end of the line the varying current passed through a receiver coil which reacted "in sympathy" reversing the original process and producing the original sound. Dom Pedro II and the world were impressed.

Scots inventors have a very erratic record as far as exploitation of ideas go. At the one extreme they miss out completely—as in the case of Lord Cochrane's father who passed on coal-gas lighting to William Murdoch and could not even make anything out of his links with Macadam to find a use for the coal tar. In the middle ground, they either opt out of the gravy train for humanitarian reasons—as Sir Alexander Fleming did with his penicillin—or they never manage to get on it—the fate of John Logie Baird and his television work. Alexander Graham Bell stands firmly at the other end of the scale. He sold his interests to big business and made a great deal of money. He went on to other work but nothing could compete with the telephone. He became a sort of father figure for US inventors—and is even shown on a stamp commemorating the Wright Brothers flight, standing patriarchically between them!

Bell never saw himself as an inventor pure and simple. "I am sure that I should never have invented the telphone if I had been an electrician. What electrician would have hit upon so mad an idea? I must confess that to this day I don't understand *how* it is possible that someone can speak in Washington and someone else hear him at the foot of the Eiffel Tower."

He was a teacher of the deaf—and while he may have made more money out of the telephone depicted on so many postage stamps, he may very well have derived more satisfaction from another event which has been honoured in this way. Stamps were issued in 1980 showing the great and unique team of Helen Keller, the prodigious deaf blind mute, and her amazing teacher, Margaret Sullivan—the greatest triumph in the history of human disability. It was a story of triumph which began when Helen's mother brought her to a bearded and kindly teacher of the deaf, with piercing eyes and a deep musical voice, who saw in the child the spark of intelligence and the thrust of determination and urged that these could be brought out by the individual attention and devotion of a companion.

James Clerk Maxwell 1831-1879

—the greatest mind to come out of Scotland

In 1845, the learned members of the Royal Society of Edinburgh heard an imaginative mathematical paper on the subject of the refraction of light in elliptically curved glass sheets. The paper was read by proxy as it were, for the writer, a schoolboy of 14, was considered too young to take the responsibility of delivering it to such an august body. It was the first public demonstration of a genius that was to develop into the greatest scientific mind ever to emanate from Scotland.

James Clerk Maxwell was born on 13 June 1831 at 14 India Street, Edinburgh—yet another product of the fertile well-to-do classes who lived in the capital's elegant Georgian New Town. His formative environment, however, was to come from another part of Scotland, the family estate at Glenair in Galloway in south-west Scotland. There he developed a love for that appealing and varied landscape that was to run alongside his passion for knowledge.

His early education by private tutor was hardly guaranteed to stimulate any latent genius. To recite the longest chapter of the Bible at eight showed that the boy had a good brain: it did little to develop it. The death of his mother when he was quite young and the cultural shock of moving at the age of ten to an Edinburgh Academy which found him rustic in the extreme combined to produce a rather reticent adolescent, but did nothing to dampen his boundless delight in experiment and investigation and the impedimenta of wires, struts and gadgets with which he probed his concepts and ideas.

He spent three years at the University of Edinburgh and then went on to Cambridge, firstly to the oldest college of Peterhouse and then to the largest of Trinity. There he impressed even those accustomed to exceptional talent. A fellow student recalled: "Hopkins (their tutor with a reputation for fostering Cambridge's brightest mathematicians) was talking to me this evening about Maxwell. He says he is unquestionably the most extraordinary man he has met in the whole range of his experience. He says it appears impossible for Maxwell to think incorrectly on physical subjects. He looks upon him as a great genius with all its eccentricities, and prophesies that one day he will shine as a light in physical science—a prophesy in which all his fellow students strenuously unite."

Maxwell lost no time in proving his tutor correct. He won the Adams' Prize offered by neighbouring college of St Johns for an explanation of the rings of Saturn—and his basic theory, novel at the time, that they consisted of swarms of particles travelling at different speeds stood up to the overwhelming body of evidence sent back by Voyager I when it passed the area in 1980.

At the age of 25 he was appointed Professor at Marischal College, Aberdeen, and it seems as if, to the lad brought up among the hills and rivers of Galloway and now living in the featureless and flat Fens, the attractions of the move were geographical as well as academic. He lost the post when Aberdeen's two universities merged in 1860, failed to get a chair at his *alma mater* in Edinburgh and eventually became Professor at Kings College, London. He resigned that post in

1865, returning to his beloved Glenair, but came out of retirement in 1871 to become Professor of Physics at Cambridge.

Maxwell was the first to put forward a theoretical concept of just how colour was produced. He used, just as modern photographic film, printing and television do, coloured filters to produce red, green and blue elements from which he built up an image. And, in deference to his roots and perhaps to the legend that it was the only thing that would beat a chameleon, he even used a piece of tartan to prove his point.

He developed a kinetic theory to explain the behaviour of gases, an astonishing triumph of boundless theoretical thinking. But his most lasting work came in the exposition of the links between electricity, magnetism and light. Just as sound is artificially limited by the performance of the human ear which can only detect a small part of the band, so light has been defined in terms of the capabilities of the human eye. Maxwell suggested that light waves existed in forms beyond those which we have detected and progressed into what were eventually extended to take in as X-rays, gamma rays, microwaves and radio waves. It was some ten years after Maxwell's work that Hertz was able to demonstrate the theory in relation to radio waves. The complementary nature of the two men's work is underlined by a stamp issued by Mexico in 1967 to mark an International Telecommunications Conference being held in Mexico City which shows the team of Maxwell and Hertz.

Over the comparative short span of his academic career, Maxwell, the gauche, kindly, reserved genius, stumbling at face-to-face explanations or teachings, but brilliant at written explanations, produced a body of thought and concept unequalled by any physical scientist except Newton. Much later, Einstein, one of the heirs of Maxwell's work, said, "It took physicists some decades to grasp the full significance of Maxwell's discovery, so bold was the leap that his genius forced upon the concepts of his fellow-workers!" When they did, they were to give the twentieth century radio and television, colour photography, printing and transmission.

He died in 1879 of cancer and is buried in Parton Old Church, near Glenair. A stained-glass window commemorates the link between the genius and that corner of Scotland.

William Ramsay 1852-1916

—the discoverer of four or five chemical elements

"To lose one parent" declared Lady Brackenbury in Wilde's play *The Importance of Being Earnest* "may be regarded as a misfortune; to lose both looks like carelessness." Of Sir William Ramsay, she might well have suggested that if to discover one chemical element may be regarded as good fortune, to discover four or five certainly looks like some sort of careful talent.

For William Ramsay, born in Glasgow in 1852 and educated at the city's university, the tracking down of those four or five elements—narrowly failing to equal Sir Humphrey Davy's admittedly more significant six—began with a question asked by someone else. John William Strutt, Lord Rayleigh, one of the leading physicists of the day, wanted to know why the density of the nitrogen obtained from the air was greater than that of the nitrogen obtained chemically.

Ramsay, Professor of Chemistry at University College London and previously Professor of Chemistry at Bristol, was becoming increasingly interested in the new branch of his subject—physical chemistry—and took up the challenge of Rayleigh's question. Rayleigh himself favoured the existence of some strange variant of nitrogen but Ramsay discovered that

G

the culprit was a hitherto unknown gas, argon, which lurked, scarce and inert, forming about one per cent of the atmosphere. The presence of this gas in "atmospheric" nitrogen and its absence in "chemical" nitrogen explained the difference in densities.

Pursuing this lead and looking for other sources of argon, Ramsay discovered helium. This introduces a hazy distinction to confuse the issue and to explain why we have said "four or five" elements. Helium was already known to exist: an Anglo-French team had stated this in 1868. But no-one had ever come across any; the discovery had been based on spectroscopic research, that is, the gas was known to exist on the sun, but had not been located on earth. We might perhaps give Ramsay half an element as a compromise.

Ramsay proceeded to track down three other of the so-called inert gases, discovering in 1898 neon, krypton and xenon, the latter present in the atmosphere in quantities of only one part in 170,000,000.

Ramsay, possessed of what one writer has called a "marvellous manipulative skill" was a doughty teacher and infectious research leader. He was knighted for his work in 1902 and received the Nobel Prize for Chemistry in 1904. There was a certain poetry in the fact that Lord Rayleigh who started it all was awarded the prize for Physics in the same year.

THE
SCOTTISH
PEN

In his delightful little book *Famous Scots*, Weir Gilmour includes under inventors, Sir Walter Scott—as the man who gave the world the historical novel, the adventure tale. It is the one literary specialisation in which Scotland leads the world. Despite the national love of Burns, the action story is the Scottish forte. The great trio of Scott (never, despite his great influence on Europe, featured on a postage stamp other than in the rather faint tribute of the music of the opera *Quentin Durward* used as the background to a stamp honouring a Belgian composer), Stevenson and Doyle may just about hold their own against the French line-up of Hugo, Dumas and Verne. When it comes to back-up support, however, the Scots win a distinct edge—and don't even have to call upon Ian Fleming whose Dundee roots provided the fortune to enable him to produce the high-living "007". Just think of a First XI that consists of *The Coral Island, Ivanhoe, The Lost World, Hound of the Baskervilles, Dr Jekyll and Mr Hyde, Treasure Island, The Thirty-nine Steps, Guns of Navarone, Kidnapped, Brigadier Gerard* and *Campbell's Kingdom* and you will see just what the opposition is up against.

At the heart of the works of the writers who have become honoured on stamps is one element common to nearly all of them: the ability to create memorable characters, from Long John Silver to Sherlock Holmes, from Dangerous Dan Magrew to Peter Pan, from Tam o' Shanter to Dr Jekyll.

Robert Burns
1759-1796

—more than a national poet

Scotland cherishes inventors—and as a result she has had more than her fair share of them. In October, 1788, one of those inventors, and no mean one at that, was facing the moment of truth on the small loch of Dalswinton to the north of Dumfries. It was Patrick Miller's first—and incidentally last—steamboat and was a success, making five knots. The event was an historic one, for when Patrick Miller, banker and dilettante, gave it up to pass on to some other fad, the man who made the engine, William Symington, took over, built the *Charlotte Dundas* and gave steamboats to the world. Scotland has forgotten Patrick Miller and his boat, but one of his crew, listed as R. Burns, continues to hold in the hearts of Scots a place unchallenged by all the explorers, inventors, soldiers or leaders.

Born on 25 January 1759, in an Alloway cottage built by his father, Robert Burns observed from the start that "man was made to mourn," seeing his father struggle on rented farms to convert great effort into small comfort. It was a struggle which the elder Burns never mastered and by 1784 he was dead leaving Robert to take on the new farm of Mossgiel.

Up to that date, Robert Burns' story was one that could have been echoed by thousands of Scottish lads, even down to the liberal and colourful sprinkling of affairs, abounding in pregnant servant girls, angry fathers and affronted kirk sessions. But into that often encountered tapestry was being woven a new, golden thread; Robert was a poet. He was educated and well read, for William Burns, throughout his tribulations, had not neglected to pay Robert into the local farmers' educational co-operative, the tutor who gave the farmers' sons a grounding in language and literature, history and geography. From this base, Robert had been able to channel his imagination and sensitivity into poetry. The contacts he made at his local debating club of Tarbolton and during visits to Irvine (to pick up tips on flax-dressing) encouraged him in his inclinations. Not even the back-breaking task of running the farm, where he and his brother Gilbert were having no more success than their father had done, could hold back Robert from building up a stock of poems, young man's poems, poems of love and despair, poems of the countryside, poems of revolt against kirk and laird. In a couple of years he had built up enough for a book and on 31 July 1786 the Kilmarnock edition of *Poems, chiefly in the Scottish Dialect* was published. It was by any standards a success. Scotland's uniquely literate countryfolk had found a new poet—and the critics were aware of a new voice, a promising champion of the Scots dialect.

Money was undoubtedly the motive behind the publication as Burns, formerly dismissed by a protective father as not the right husband for his daughter, Jean Armour, was now being required to marry the girl in view of pressing changes in her condition. Burns thought of going to Jamaica with Jean and needed the passage money. The reception of the Kilmarnock Edition hinted that there might be more than his fare in the poetry business and Burns, leaving his native county for the first time in his life, set off for Edinburgh where fame and fortune lay in wait.

Dr Blacklock, the blind poet and critic was, like some latter-day John the Baptist, preparing the way for the new poet, with enthusiastic appraisals of the poems in the influential *Edinburgh Magazine*.

Burns' reception in Edinburgh was quite extraordinary. On the one hand the literary and social circles lionized him; on the other hand the lawyers' apprentices and their friends took him into their circle just as his friends in the Tarbolton bachelors' club had done. He had arrived.

At one of the many gatherings where he held sway, dominant in conversation, magnetic in the reading of his poetry, Burns was observed by a lad of fifteen: "He was of manners rustic, not clownish. The eye alone indicated the poetical character and temperament; it was large and of a dark cast and literally glowed when he spoke with feeling or interest." That boy, Walter Scott, who figures in the stories of so many of the Scots covered in this book, perhaps owes his own passion for Scotland to the works of the man he saw across a crowded salon.

The *Edinburgh Edition* of Burns' poems hit the streets in 1787 and Burns was to collect as much as £500 from the proceeds. He made a number of short tours of Scotland, returned to Edinburgh, writing little poems but carrying on a Sylvander-and-Clarinda relationship with a married but neglected Edinburgh lady, Mrs Maclehose.

He returned to the farm of Mossgiel with his £500, lent Gilbert nearly £200 and settled down to the business of succeeding where his father had failed. The still faithful Jean Armour, underlining the point made by her twins of 1786 produced another child in 1788 and succeeded in dragging Burns to the altar. He moved on to another farm at Ellisland in Dumfriesshire and tried to supplement farming with the steady income of an exciseman but the strain proved too great and at the end of 1791 he gave up farming for good and moved to Dumfries. His pen was prolific, and he wrote to the last, producing a staggering range of work from the satirical to the sentimental, from songs to bawdy poems and including the finest comic poem in English literature, "Tam o' Shanter" and the words sung more often than any others, "Auld Lang Syne." He died of rheumatic fever in 1796.

Poets do not get on to other people's postage stamps merely by writing great poetry. Byron made the grade as a freedom fighter rather than as a literary figure. Burns is acknowledged on the stamps of the Soviet Union and Romania as a poet who championed the cause of the common man—and perhaps the poem "A Man's a man for a' that" provided the biggest boost of all for that rôle.

For Scots, however, the attraction of the poet is much more complex than that. He gave dignity and standing to the language they spoke, and treated it not as some comic variant of English but as a powerful, poignant, musical, magical, dignified tongue. He gave voice to Scottish values, put Scottish songs into words and made Scottish words sing.

Above all he was a Scot—and his internationalism derived, as the best internationalism usually does, from a passionate conviction of where his own roots lay. He could write from his farm at Ellisland in March 1790: "I have often read *The Spectator* but with a certain regret for it is so thoroughly and entirely English—alas I have often said to myself, what are the advantages Scotland reaps from this so-called Union that can counterbalance the annihilation of her independence and her very name." Today, a similar letter to *The Scotsman* would be met with charges of racialism and parochialism.

The combination of creativity and imagination, gentleness and anger, praise and scorn, reverence and rudeness, which make up Burns' Scottishness has converted him into a national poet who has no equivalent elsewhere in literature. Shakespeare may hold the title of the poet who has had most *written* about him; Burns is in undisputed possession of the title of the poet who has had the most words *spoken* about him, and every year around 25 January in convivial gatherings not just in Scotland but in the many lands to which Scots went to find a new life, the gap between Burns and his rivals will yawn still wider.

Lord Byron
1788-1824

—the poet who died
a hero

Angry and tearful from the news, the adolescent Alfred Tennyson fled to the private depths of a wood and hacked on a rock "Byron is dead." He was not alone in feeling that, in the death of that tragic and exiled poet, he and his generation had lost a voice, that what had happened in dank Missolonghi in the fight for Greek freedom mattered to the youth of Britain. Perhaps, recently, we have come close to understanding just what Tennyson and his contemporaries felt when we were confronted with the murder of John Lennon, martyr in the cause of peace, as Byron was a casualty in the search for his generation's grails of liberalism and liberty.

Eight years earlier, Byron had been hounded from Britain by a society that did not scandalise easily, but was rocked by the extravagant arrogance of the poet's extremely public private life, by the free-thinking scepticism of his verse, but most of all by the frightening aggression of his sex life which spilt over from an accepted blend of marriage and adultery into dark tales of incest with his half-sister and of homosexuality.

If Byron had ever wanted to plead mitigating circumstances for his social crimes, he certainly had them in abundance. His father, Captain Mad Jack Byron, came from a line of fast-living rakes one might scour in vain in search of a white sheep. He had married in 1785 Catherine Gordon of the Aberdeenshire estate of Gight, whose attractions to the creditor-pursued Captain were primarily financial. By the time she had tied up her money in a form that would keep it out of the clutches of Mad Jack, Gight Castle had been sold and most of the cash thrown to the wolfish creditors who were pursuing Captain Byron, leaving him to flee to France. Catherine followed, dutifully, to nurse her step-daughter back to health, but, ill at ease in Paris, she returned to Britain and took lodgings in Holles Street, just off London's Oxford Street. There on 22 January 1788, a son was born. It was a Tuesday and the baby had to wait a few days to meet his father as Captain Byron only visited his wife on Sundays. This was not for any pious reason, merely that on that day debtors were safe from prosecution.

From the start it was clear that the baby had a severely deformed foot. Catherine consulted a fellow-Scot, John Hunter, one of the two Lanarkshire brothers who dominated London's medical and surgical scene. He designed a special shoe, but declared that the foot could never be completely cured.

Catherine did not stay long in London and moved with her son, named George Gordon after her father, to Aberdeen, close to her family homeland.

It was here that young George Gordon Byron was to spend his first ten years; later he was to claim:

"But I am half a Scot by birth and bred
A whole one."

The Scottish influences on his life were significant, and were primarily related to liberalism, nature, reading and literature and, surprisingly for Presbyterian Scotland, sex.

His mother, for all her pride in ancestry—"as haughty as Lucifer with her descent from the Stuarts", claimed her son—brought him a liberal element tinged with good Scottish egalitarianism. This was to counteract the aristocratic streak in Byron's makeup and lead him to make his first speech in the House of Lords in defence of the Nottinghamshire weavers who had broken up the frames which threatened their jobs, and his final one in defence of the Radical Cartwright, effectively scotching any thoughts Byron might have had of a political career.

His many visits to the Scottish countryside and in particular to the area around Ballater aroused his interest in nature, while his lessons and reading at the Aberdeen schools opened up a new world of adventure and history, of stirring deeds and worthy heroes.

But perhaps the two greatest influences on his early life came from his two Scottish nurses. Agnes Gray instilled in him a Calvinistic awareness of sin and evil and introduced him to the great cadences of the Old Testament language, while her younger sister, May, brought home even more forcibly the reality of punishment and the more confusing reality of sex.

None of these influences, however, could begin to compare with the handicap of the club foot. The talented sensitive boy hated that foot and started early in life a never-ending campaign to replace the image of the poor deformed boy with anything that could push it into the background: the athlete, the rake, the lecher, the poet, the hero, the liberator.

Even on the physical plane he strove to show that he could out-box, out-run, out-swim luckier boys. At Harrow, he played cricket, taking part in the first Eton-Harrow game in 1805, but swimming above all other sports enabled him to forget the lameness. From his early days in the Dee and Don, he developed as a very talented swimmer, chalking up accomplishments in later life from the Tagus to the Hellespont. He wrote, with feeling:

> And I have loved thee, Ocean! and my joy
> Of youthful sports was on thy breast to be
> Borne, like thy bubbles, onwards; from a boy
> I wantoned with thy breakers.

The water was to play a tragic part in his life as well. One of his University friends, Skinner Matthews, drowned in the weeds of the Cam, while his greatest friend, Shelley, was to be washed up on the beach of Viareggio leaving Byron to cremate the fish-gnawed corpse.

Byron's Scottish life came to an abrupt end at the age of ten, when his grandfather died. His father, Mad Jack, having passed on some years earlier, George became the Sixth Lord

Byron. He moved south to the family estate at Newstead in Nottinghamshire and, as befitted a young "English" aristocrat, passed on to boarding school at Harrow and to University at Cambridge. These prepared him for the life of a wild man-about-town in London, with a capacity for spending which far outstripped his capacity for earning. Alongside a slowly emerging literary skill went a speedily developing reputation for torrid affairs.

He went on the Grand Tour of Europe in 1809, tacking on a little bit of Asia for good measure, and never recovered from the effects. He fell deeply in love with Greece and Turkey and, from those landscapes littered with evidence of stirring deeds, he developed the Byronic hero, in his *Childe Harolde's Pilgrimage*, written on the Tour. He was never to leave his public in any doubt that he wanted them to associate himself with the heroes he created, a sort of brooding cross between Hamlet and Robin Hood.

He came back to Britain, determined to become a literary figure. On 10 March 1813, John Murray published *Childe Harold's Pilgrimage* in London and as Byron reported, "I awoke one morning and found myself famous."

The combination of the poet's outspoken lines, undeniable physical beauty, and, although he may not have agreed, lameness proved irresistible to the ladies of London and further afield and his rake's progress of seduction was well on the way to creating the outcry which led to him leaving England for the last time in 1816. Crowds swarmed to see him depart from Dover with, we are told, ladies of high birth disguising themselves as chambermaids to catch a last glimpse of the Bad Lord Byron. They would no doubt have tutted a chorus of "I told you so" if they were ever to read the comment of one of Byron's companions, Dr John Polidori, that when they arrived at Ostend, "As soon as he reached his room, Lord Byron fell like a thunderbolt upon the chambermaid."

On this prolonged one-way Grand Tour Byron spent most of his time in Italy, but by the end of 1823 the magnet of the

Greeks' struggle for emancipation from their Turkish overlords had lured Byron to the country where he was to die. He had already dallied with the forces of liberalism and independence in Italy, in the form of the underground Carbonari. The Greek Committee of emigrés working from London realised that Lord Byron, whose literary fame had grown during his years on the Continent with the publication of later parts of *Childe Harold* and such poems as "The Prisoner of Chillon," "Manfred," "Mazzeppa" and "Don Juan," would be able to contribute to their cause in terms of money, morale and propaganda and invited him to Greece.

Despite his misgivings about the gap between the merits of the cause and the bickering of the protagonists, Byron could not resist the chance to become a liberating hero. He arrived in Missolonghi on 5 January 1824 and was "received like a Delivering Angel." With an entourage of Suliotes (the exiled warriors from the fastnesses of Albania who were to him the symbol of fierce independence), he tried to impose some sort of unity upon the freedom-fighters, but after a few months in the swamp-girt town the already weakened Byron fell ill and on 19 April 1824 he died to the noise of a violent storm. A few years earlier he had expressly stated that his body was not to be taken back to England:

> I am sure my bones would not rest in an English grave
> or my clay mix with the earth of that country. I believe
> that thought would drive me mad on my deathbed could I
> suppose that any of my friends would be base enough to
> convey my carcass back to your soil.

He seems to have relented in the intervening years and the body was returned to England to be buried in July at the village of Hucknall Torkard near Nottingham. When the body was being prepared for the long journey home, the Greeks requested that some part of the body should remain in Greece and the lungs of the poet-hero rest in the Church of San Spiridone at Missolonghi.

Robert Louis Stevenson 1850-1894

—"Tusitala"—the teller of tales

John Bartholomew, third in a line of Edinburgh engravers, was a wizard with maps, and few corners of the globe had escaped his attention at one time or another. Now he was given a map with no latitude or longitude, a map he was to credit to another, one Mr W. Bones, a map to be dated nearly a century and half earlier, a map of an island that never was: and all to the instructions of another Edinburgh man, nearly twenty years his junior. The map was to appear in print more times and be studied by more people than any other map produced by Bartholomews or any other mapmaker; it was a map of that treasure island at the centre of a story that would fascinate millions, appear in countless forms and many languages and even tempt the great Walt Disney away from cartoon characters to his first conventional adventure film.

The creator of the magical island was born in Edinburgh near the Water of Leith at 8 Howard Place on 13 November 1850. Like John Bartholomew, he seemed to have been born into a craft as well as into a family, in his case not map engraving but the design and construction of lighthouses. A weak and feeble disposition in childhood diverted young Stevenson from following in that exacting and robust profession and paradoxically provided him with the alternative. His years of childhood sicknesses were spent with books and toys, which stretched his imagination and tempted him to writing. In particular, his Victorian cut-out theatre, with backdrops and characters gave him an essentially dramatic outlook on life. He could never see a landscape, rustic or urban, without getting an urge to populate it, to place characters and deeds on the stage, before the heathered hill, the bustling port, the claustrophobic close or the island beach.

Stevenson came under the strong influence of his nurse, Alison Cunningham. His early literary efforts were enthusiastic and he relished experimenting in a variety of styles, developing the superb control of language that characterised his writing throughout his life.

The settings in which he grew up had especially lasting effects on him; the elegant New Town, the cramped and mysterious Old Town of Edinburgh, the gentle manse at Colinton where Stevenson visited his grandfather, and the village of Swanston, nesting under the rolling Pentland Hills.

As was expected of a young man from Edinburgh's middle classes he entered the city's University, a period in which he missed classes and pitched with zeal into the underworld of Edinburgh, setting off as if to overtake Burns, John Paul Jones and Byron as far as sexual excesses were concerned, a dandy, velvet-clad eccentric, frequent visitor to the bawdy houses, a Bohemian in the capital of respectability. He wanted to be a writer, and devoted to the learning of that craft far more energy than to the business of getting a degree. The slack, distracted university student was a ruthless disciplinarian as far as his writing was concerned. After a long spell of much being written and nothing being published, he began slowly to make an impression on the London scene, with essays in the *Cornhill Magazine*.

The Scottish climate continued to prove painful to the weak, illness-prone writer and the rest of his life was to be dictated by a quest for the ideal spot in which to endure his disability. He travelled to France, to California (in pursuit of his future wife whom he had met in France), to Switzerland, to Bournemouth, back to the States and finally, as fame and a little fortune came, to the South Pacific.

The inspiration of the changing settings produced a wide

variety of work from Stevenson and the titles that were to make him famous flowed not without difficulty but always with his superb distinctive style. *Travels with a Donkey, Treasure Island*, written to amuse his stepson, *The Black Arrow, Kidnapped, Catriona, The Master of Ballantrae*, the tingling *Dr Jekyll and Mr Hyde*.

The books were never best-sellers in the modern sense of providing the writer with a fortune. To keep the income flowing, Stevenson had to keep the writing flowing—at one stage, having lost his voice, he dictated fiction on his fingers by the dumb alphabet. In the summer of 1888 Stevenson began his venture with his wife, family and the affiliated "clan" to the Pacific islands on the chartered yacht *Casco*. In 1890 he and Fanny made their home, Vailima, on one of the Samoan islands. Here they lived for more than four years and here Stevenson produced some of his finest work.

Then in 1894, as Edinburgh stoked up her fires in the numbing cold of midwinter and poured out the sepia smoke that earned her the nickname Auld Reekie, a world away, after a long very hot day at the height of the Pacific summer, one of Edinburgh's most famous sons fell dead in front of his shaving mirror. The strange bond of birthplace and deathplace was underlined by the fact that on his finger he wore a ring, carved not by an unknown craftsman but by a Samoan chief, engraved with the word *Tusitala*, "The Teller of Tales," while on his desk lay *The Weir of Hermiston*, the unfinished manuscript of a novel of passsion, love, justice and duty set in the bleak northern capital he loved and in the countryside that rolled southwards to England.

LUXEMBOURG

6F

A. GRAHAM BELL

1876 – 1976 – CENTENAIRE DE LA
PREMIÈRE LIAISON TÉLÉPHONIQUE

100TH ANNIVERSARY OF ALEXANDER GRAHAM BELL

1/2c

Bell's First Telephone

GRENADA GRENADINES

ÉIRE

15

AN CHÉAD GHLAOCH TELEFÓIN 1876

الجمهورية الاسلامية الموريتانية

100ÈME ANNIVERSAIRE DE LA 1ÈRE LIAISON TÉLÉPHONIQUE

POSTES

10 UM

REPUBLIQUE ISLAMIQUE DE MAURITANIE

PHONE · A. GRAHAM BELL (1847 - 1922)

15 S

100e ANNIVERSAIRE DE L'INVENTION DU TÉ

RÉPUBLIQUE DE GUINÉE

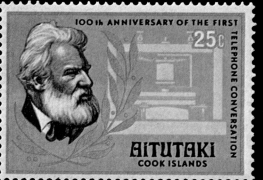

100th ANNIVERSARY OF THE FIRST

25c

TELEPHONE CONVERSATION

AITUTAKI
COOK ISLANDS

REPUBLIQUE TOGOLAISE

105 F

POSTE AÉRIENNE

A.G. BELL · 1847 - 1922

CENTENAIRE DE LA 1ère LIAISON TELEPHONIQUE

INDIA

ऐलिग्ज़ेंडर ग्रैम बेल 1847-1922
ALEXANDER GRAHAM BELL

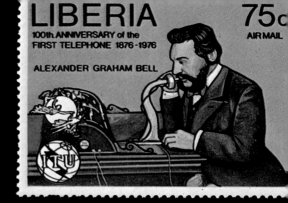

LIBERIA

75c

100th ANNIVERSARY of the
FIRST TELEPHONE 1876-1976

AIR MAIL

ALEXANDER GRAHAM BELL

ITU

1·00

ශ්‍රී ලංකා
இலங்கை
SRI LANKA   TELEPHONE CENTENARY

100TH ANNIVERSARY OF
ALEXANDER GRAHAM BELL

1/2c

GRENADA

ALEXANDER GRAHAM BELL

TELEPHONE CENTENARY 1876-1976

1905

20c

Swaziland

1976 CENTENARY OF FIRST
TELEPHONE TRANSMISSION
ALEXANDER GRAHAM BELL

10t

Malaŵi

3 Ft
ALEXANDER G. BELL
100 ÉVES
AZ ELSŐ TÁVBESZÉLŐ ÖSSZEKÖTTETÉS
1876-1976
MAGYAR POSTA
1976
VERTEL JÓZSEF

GRAHAM BELL
1876 MONACO 1976
0.80 PREMIÈRE LIAISON TELEPHONIQUE

100TH ANNIVERSARY OF THE FIRST TELEPHONE CONVERSATION
GRAHAM BELL
1876-1976
BAHAMAS
21c

POSTES 37F
G·BELL POLYNESIE FRANCAISE
1876~CENTENAIRE DE LA 1RE LIAISON TELEPHONIQUE~1976

CENTENARIO DEL TELEFONO
3 PTA CORREOS ESPAÑA
F.N.M.T.

75th ANNIVERSARY OF FIRST MOTORIZED AIRPLANE
O. AND W.WRIGHT WITH A.G.BELL,1910
REPUBLIC OF MALDIVES
20 L

NOBELPRIS 1904
RAMSAY
PAVLOV
SVERIGE 40

$e^{\ln N} = N$
LEY DE NAPIER
AEREO
25
CENTAVOS

NICARAGUA

LAS 10 FORMULAS MATEMATICAS QUE CAMBIARON LA FAZ DE LA TIERRA

$$\nabla^2 E = Ku \frac{\delta^2 E}{c^2 \, \delta t^2}$$
LEY DE MAXWELL
CORREO
2
CORDOBAS

NICARAGUA

LAS 10 FORMULAS MATEMATICAS QUE CAMBIARON LA FAZ DE LA TIERRA

80 ¢
AEREO
MEXICO
1967
HERTZ   MAXWELL
PLAN MUNDIAL DE TELECOMUNICACIONES
PRUNEDA

'Treasure Island'

'ROBERT·LOUIS STEVENSON
'TUSITALA' 1894 : 19.

7 sene
SAMOA I SISIFO

10 c US CY

R.VIRGIN ISLANDS

GIBRALTAR

2/- GENERAL ELIOTT 1717-1790   GREAT SIEGE 1779-1783

GIBRALTAR

REPUBLIQUE DE CÔTE D'IVOIRE   100 F

BICENTENAIRE DES ETATS-UNIS 1776-1976

MARIN AMERICAIN

JOHN PAUL JONES

PERU

82 · 19

LORD COCHRANE

7 CENTAVOS

LIT C. FABBRI-LIMA

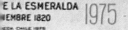

CIMIENTO DE LORO COCHRANE   BICENTENARIO DEL NACIMIENTO DE LORO COCHRANE   BICENTENARIO DEL NAC

CHILE $1   CHILE $1

E LA ESMERALDA 1975   1775   BLINDADO COCHRANE 1975   1775   DESTRUCT

NIEMBRE 1820   26 DICIEMBRE 1874   26 J

10c GRENADA

American Revolution
Bicentennial 1776-1976

"I Have Not Yet Begun to Fight"
John Paul Jones

CHILE CORREOS

1810
1910

ALMIRANTE COCHRANE

10 DIEZ PESOS

AMERICAN BANK NOTE CO. N.Y.

RHODESIA MATABELELAND

1893-1968

POSTAGE 1'6

ALLAN WILSON

ПОЧТА СССР 1979

ДЖОН
МАКЛИН
1879~1923

4 к

JAMES CONNOLLY 1868 1916

EIRE 1/-

0.40

ISRAEL

LORD BALFOUR

יובל
להצהרת
בלפור
BALFOUR
DECLARATION
1917-1967

ישראל

1759 1796

Роберт Бёрнс
Великий национальный
поэт Шотландии

Почта СССР 40 коп.

MARILE ANIVERSĂRI CULTURALE - 1959

R. BURNS

1759-1796

55 BANI POSTA
R.P. ROMÎNA

Robert W Service   Sam McGee

Canada postes 8
postage

ΕΛΛΑΣ ΛΟΡΔΟΣ ΒΥΡΩΝ 1824-1974
HELLAS

ΔP. 4.50

1824 ΕΛΛΑΣ 1924

LORD BYRON

80 ΛΕΠΤΑ 80

BRADBURY, WILKINSON & CO. LTD. LONDON

ΛΟΡΔΟΣ ΒΥΡΩΝ 1824-1974

ΕΛΛΑΣ HELLAS ΔP. 2.50

1188 BYRON 1824

5 f
LÉGIPOSTA MAGYARORSZÁG

INTERPOL 50
ANIVERSARIO

LOS DOCE DETECTIVES MAS
FAMOSOS DE LA FICCION

A. CONAN DOYLE

221-b. Baker St.

Sherlock Holmes

2.00 Aéreo NICARAGUA
DE LA RUE DE COLOMBIA

JAMES I 1603—1625 35c

BARBUDA

Nº 25

RED RIVER SETTLEMENT · 1812

5¢ CANADA

SELKIRK

LA COLONIE DE LA RIVIÈRE ROUGE · 1812

$1

Bahamas
THE COUNTRY OF 700 ISLANDS
SALUTES A GOOD NEIGHBOUR

1910 NEWFOUNDLAND 1910
POSTAGE
ONE CENT

1 1

KING JAMES I.
WHO GRANTED CHARTER
TO GUY

𝕴Barbados 45c

350th Anniversary of the Charter to Carlisle

Charles I   Earl of Carlisle

35c   CHARLES I
1625—1649

BARBUDA

Nº 26

80th Birthday of
Her Majesty Queen Elizabeth
The Queen Mother
4th August 1980
H.M. COMMISSIONER IN
$3·00 ANGUILLA

50¢
COOK ISLANDS

80th BIRTHDAY OF
H.M. Queen Elizabeth
The Queen Mother
4th AUGUST 1980
PITCAIRN ISLANDS 50¢

$1
PENRHYN
NORTHERN COOK ISLANDS

বাংলাদেশ BANGLADESH

80th Birthday of
Her Majesty Queen Elizabeth
The Queen Mother
৳১৫
POSTAGE TK 15

$2.50

80th Birthday of
Her Majesty Queen Elizabeth
The Queen Mother
4th August 1980

COMMONWEALTH OF
DOMINICA

0,80 $ · U.1.ს.ს.

80th. Birthday

POSTE ERITREA

of the
Queen Mother

ELIZABETH II CORONATION 1953-1978

英皇太后八十華誕
一九八零年八月四日
80th BIRTHDAY OF
H. M. Queen Elizabeth
The Queen Mother
4th AUGUST 1980

E II R
$1·30

HONG KONG 香港

E II R · ROYAL VISIT 1975 · E II R

JERSEY 20 p

COURVOISIER S.A.

80th Birthday of Queen Elizabeth the Queen Mother—4th August 1980

$2·50

REDONDA

80th Birthday of
Her Majesty Queen Elizabeth
The Queen Mother
4th August 1980

$ 2.50

SAINT
LUCIA

80th Birthday of
H.M.Queen Elizabeth
The Queen Mother

5s

LESOTHO

TUVALU EⅡR

50c   50c

80th. Birthday
Her Majesty Queen Elizabeth
The Queen Mother

M1.

ROYAL VISIT 1947
2d   BASUTOLAND   2d

1900-1980

80th Birthday of
H.M.Queen Elizabeth
The Queen Mother

LESOTHO

M1.

80th Birthday of
H.M.Queen Elizabeth
The Queen Mother

10s

LESOTHO

$1.10

LA COPA MUNDIAL-1978
Franz Beckenbauer
Denis Law
50 CTS AEREO
NICARAGUA

Sir David & Lady Gill at the Site of their Living Tent
Ascension Island 12p
Centenary of the visit of Professor Gill to Ascension Island

STATE OF
NORTH BORNEO
BRITISH PROTECTORATE
4
POSTAGE & REVENUE
FOUR CENTS
4

SIR JOHN ALCOCK, SIR ARTHUR WHITTEN BROWN
1919-1979
100F
REPUBLIQUE DU NIGER
VASARHELYI

JOHORE
POSTAGE & REVENUE
8 CENTS

1 DH.
Jim CLARK
POSTAGE
AJMAN

CORREOS DE CHILE
30 CTS
ROBINSON CRUSOE
ARCHIPIELAGO DE JUAN FERNANDEZ
CASA DE MONEDA DE CHILE

Arthur Conan Doyle 1859-1930

—blueprint for a detective

If practical Glasgow gave the world its most famous real detective in the person of Allan J. Pinkerton, the more thoughtful Edinburgh gave it its most famous literary detective in the even more believable character of Mr Sherlock Holmes.

The great detective came to life in 1887 and, if present popularity is anything to go by, looks like hurtling past his hundredth birthday with no signs of mortality. The ever-so-English Holmes was the product of an Edinburgh doctor with an Irish pedigree.

Arthur Conan Doyle was born in Picardy Place, Edinburgh on 22 May 1859, grandson of a political cartoonist, nephew of one of *Punch's* most distinguished caricaturists and, more significantly for the young lad, son of a civil servant, Charles Doyle, whose income failed to keep pace with his offspring. Arthur was brought up with no frills and flounces and developed into a bluff belligerent boy with a love of books. He travelled south of the Border for a Roman Catholic education, and after an interlude on the Continent, he, in the words of Hesketh Pearson, "returned to poverty in Edinburgh. His father was still painting, still in the clouds, still producing children and still earning £240 a year."

He entered Edinburgh University in October 1876 and set off on what he described as "a long weary grind at botany, chemistry, anatomy, physiology and a whole list of subjects many of which have a very indirect bearing on the art of curing." Along with the rudiments of medicine, he acquired at first hand experience of some Edinburgh characters who were to appear in his works, carrying but the thinnest of disguises.

Doyle's medical career got off to a series of rather unusual

H

jobs, including ship's surgeon on a West African cargo-ship and on a whaler, but he eventually settled down to some conventional practices at Southsea and London.

From these bases, he began his assault on Britain's reading public. Doyle was to write some first-rate historical novels, notably *The White Company, Micah Clarke* and the ebullient *Brigadier Gerard*; and in *The Lost World* he produced a classic adventure story. But without question, the character with which he is inextricably related is the strange, haunting, almost infallible Sherlock Holmes.

Holmes was not the first deductive detective to appear in literature. Many years earlier, Edgar Allan Poe had produced in Auguste Dupin, a prototype who, as far as crime-solving was concerned, even outpointed Holmes by solving a *real* murder on the basis of newspaper reports that were available to everyone else! The magic of Holmes was the creation of a character who became more real than any other creation in English, and perhaps even world literature. Not even the extravagant deeds done by him in deduction or disguises could make him seem unreal, witness the numbers of tourists who still hunt for 221b Baker Street, the home of the world's greatest detective.

Ever since Doyle revealed his creation, his rivals have realised that here was a character who was not just a device for solving a mystery but had somehow developed into a flesh-and-blood person. Nearly every succeeding writer of detective fiction has tried to recreate the spell, festooning their detectives with all sorts of idiosyncrasies: Holmes played the violin, so they make their detective grow orchids or moustaches. He had the trusty Watson, so their detective must also have a never absent assistant. He draws on a thoughful pipe, their detectives take snuff, drink exotic fruit cordials, suck lollipops, roll their own cigarettes. But for all the benefits of the Doyle blue-print, no fictional detective has managed to supplant Holmes. When the *Ellery Queen Magazine*, beloved of mystery buffs, submitted a questionnaire to readers to name ten top detectives, the answers produced the expected range from Charlie Chan to Philip Marlow, from Father Brown to Hercule Poirot, from Nero Wolfe to Inspector Maigret. Only one name appeared on every single questionnaire: Sherlock Holmes—and when Nicaragua came to issue the ten top detectives in a 1972 series of stamps to mark the fiftieth anniversary of Interpol, Conan Doyle's creation was given pride of place on the top-value stamp.

The genial all-rounder Doyle could never reconcile himself to one or even two roles. The doctor-writer was also a would-be politician (failing to win a seat in Edinburgh in 1900 and at Hawick in 1905), a dauntless patriot (he wrote a history of the Boer War and a defence of the conduct of the British soldiers) and an ever-enthusiastic sportsman, playing cricket, football and, above all, golf, and even introducing ski-ing to Switzerland. Scotland's greatest and most successful dilettante was knighted in 1902. He was a prolific traveller, lecturer, and experimenter.

It was perhaps his enthusiasm for new causes and pastimes that led him to the spiritualism that dominated the latter years of his life. He was stricken down by angina at the end of 1929, but despite warnings continued a vigorous public programme. He died on 7 July 1930; his last public duty was to support a deputation to the Home Secretary urging the repeal of an act passed more than two hundred years earlier by his witch-hating fellow Scot, James VI and I, which was being used to attack spiritualist mediums.

Robert Service
1874-1958

—Canada's Kipling of the Cold

At the end of the nineteenth century, travellers making their way to Dawson City, chief town in Canada's Yukon, completed the last leg of their journey by climbing up 12,000 steps hacked in the solid ice. Dawson City must have had something very special to make the journey worthwhile, and those steps worth the cutting. That something was gold.

The Yukon Territory had been carved out of Canada's Mackenzie district in order to administer the rush that followed the discovery of gold in the Klondike in 1896. The first wave consisted of the prospectors, closely followed into a harsh and often fatal environment by the rag, tag and bobtail of supplies and services, hotel-owners, shop-keepers, butchers, gamblers, ladies of ill repute, doctors, lawmen and, at the end of the long line of hopefuls, a poet.

The poet, heavily disguised as a banker in his new coonskin coat, was Robert Service, the one person who was to catch the spirit and ballyhoo, the people and the legends, the deeds dirty and daring, of that brief period of history and to share it with the people who never knew it and to pass it on to posterity.

Robert Service was born in Preston, in the north of England, in 1874. As a small child he moved to Kilwinning in Ayrshire and was brought up by his aunts. Romantic dreams of going off to sea were modified—he was sent into the office of a shipping firm—but the firm went bankrupt. The realistic Robert took a philosophic view of the situation and decided to go into a bank "because they have lots of money and I'll be sure of my pay."

In 1889, he joined, before the official age of sixteen, the Commercial Bank of Scotland at Stobcross, Glasgow. The duties were not, when compared with those inflicted on the youth of other Scots featured in this book, particularly onerous and he was able to indulge in reading, and the writing of verse. He wrote, "As soon as I discovered that rhyming presented no difficulty I began to exploit my gift." He participated in amateur dramatics and took evening classes at Glasgow University in English literature. Promotion six years later, in 1895 did not have the effect of confirming Service as a banker; it merely offered him the chance to save up enough money to fulfil at last those youthful dreams of his, or more specifically, to go cattle ranching in Canada. He amassed the passage money and set off, just a year after his promotion. He arrived in Canada with £5 in his pocket and made the long, numbing journey by wooden-seated train across the width of the largest country in the British Empire. He did everything except cattle ranching, travelling the length of the West coast from Vancouver to Mexico, digging ore, blasting rock, picking oranges, felling trees and even tending the garden in a house of ill-repute. He may very well be the only man of this last occupation to be honoured on a postage stamp.

He had left Scotland to find a life more exciting than banking. Perversely it was banking that opened up for him his great adventure. He still had, presumably rather the worse for wear, a testimonial from his manager at Stobcross, speaking of his "virtues, willingness, industry, and intelligence." This smoothed his way into the Imperial Bank of Canada, into branches in Vancouver, Victoria and Kamloops. In 1904, he was sent to the frontiers of the Imperial Bank's Empire, to the branch at Whitehorse in the Yukon.

He arrived at the end of the long Gold Rush, by train rather than by dog sledge. He pitched into the social life and responsibilities as befitted a young bachelor bank manager. His recitations of Kipling and his own work made him a welcome performer at the soirées of respectable Whitehorse society. Asked for something special for a Church Social, he realised that he had to write verse that was "not foreign but about our own bit of earth." He realised that "here was history being made and nobody was recording it . . . a veritable mine absolutely untouched and waiting to be staked."

Walking one Saturday night amid the noisy Whitehorse saloons, he hit on the line "A bunch of the boys were whooping it up" and from that single line grew "The Shooting of Dan McGrew," a voice for the Yukon and a poet for Canada.

There was no looking back for Robert Service. He produced a stream of Yukon verses, simple, strong and rhythmic, with stories of men and women, weak, strong, ruthless, frail, dedicated, venal, inspired. The verses went down well in Whitehorse, although not perhaps at the Church Social.

A Christmas bonus of a hundred dollars tempted Service to try to get the verses published. He sent them off to a Toronto publisher and, received instead of a bill a letter asking if the poet would "allow us to publish 1700 copies of your poems." The result was *Songs of a Sourdough* never, it seems, out of print since the first edition and, if the libraries of Edinburgh are anything to go by, with a steady demand even in the 1980s.

Service became a local celebrity and royalties at $4000 a year handsomely overtook his bank salary at $900 a year. Service was promoted to Dawson City in time to get a few of the stories that still echoed in the minds of the old timers.

In 1909 he resigned from the bank and three years later resigned from the Yukon, off to take his writing talent elsewhere. He became a war correspondent, covering the Greek-Turkish War of 1912 for the *Toronto Daily Star.* When the Great War broke out he tried to join the Seaforth Highlanders. The forty-year-old poet was able to disguise his grey hair but not his varicose veins. He became an ambulance driver and war correspondent, and spent the years between the Wars writing poetry and novels. He married a French girl and settled in a villa in Brittanny where he died in 1958.

Canada honoured Service with a stamp depicting "The Cremation of Sam McGee," one of the classics from his Yukon period. The freak encounter with the world of the Gold Rush had made it possible for Service to become a bestseller. He never had any great illusions about his merits: "I tried to avoid any literary quality—verse not poetry—something the schoolboy or the man in the pub would quote." He did, however, have more talent than his reputation would suggest. He spoke with a speck of truth when he claimed to have "been crucified on the cross of Dan McGrew." He left at his death a balanced, bland obituary. More suitable might be another verse of his:

> It's true my tummy is concave,
> My hair no more is wavy.
> But if I've one foot in the grave
> The other's in the gravy.

FIGHTERS—MAINLY FOR FREEDOM

Lord Byron features on the stamps of Greece, Hungary, Italy and the Soviet Union not as a result of his literary or amatory exploits but because of his links with the cause of Greek national freedom. With the Scots' unrivalled reputation for military leadership it is not surprising that he has plenty of company on that particular road to philatelic fame. Indeed, national liberation movements seem something of a Scottish speciality; if they were not extending the frontiers of the British Empire, they were hard at work dismembering those of the Spanish, Portuguese or Turkish Empire.

The Scottish military tradition goes back far beyond the nineteenth-century nationalist struggles, however, Scottish military men have provided despots or insurgents throughout the known globe with the best and most advanced fighting and leadership skills for many centuries. They have led armies with distinction on a thousand battlefields, for causes unknown and in places unpronounceable in their native Scotland—and have done this with a uniquely Scottish blend of aggression, experience and moral professionalism that has never been easy to find in the dangerous world of mercenary fighters.

Often the sons of the Scottish fighters continued the tradition for generations. The Browne family provided generals for Austria, the German States and Russia; the Douglas family gave Scandinavia a number of military leaders; in the great Napoleonic Wars, the French side contained in the Duke of Tarente, one of Bonaparte's most distinguished marshals—Etienne Jacques Joseph Alexandre Macdonald, a relative of Bonnie Prince Charlie's Flora. Arrayed against the French in the defence of Russia was the General Barclay de Tolly, scion of the Nairnshire family of Barclay.

This section contains a couple of individuals who are fighters in the strictly figurative sense, but for the most part they are military and naval men of action, representatives of the tradition of effective and reliable leadership in war.

When you have read the stories of how they came to be honoured on the stamps of other nations, you will have some idea of what the Scottish fighters had to offer. One extra element emerges from the career of Alexander Dow, as yet not honoured on a stamp.

In the middle of the eighteenth century the globe-trotting Alexander Carlisle came across his fellow Scot, Dow, who as commander of the forces of the Great Mogul and personal guard to the potentate, was arguably the most powerful Scot in the world. Carlisle suggested that Dow was in an ideal position to eliminate the Mogul and move up a place. "When I asked him" recorded the traveller, "what prevented him from yielding to that temptation he gave me this memorable answer: that it was on reflecting what his school fellows at Dunbar would think of him for being guilty of such an action."

George Augustus Eliott 1717-1790

—shot at for forty-three months

In 1777, George Augustus Eliott was approaching his sixtieth birthday and no doubt looking forward to a well-deserved retirement from the strenuous business of soldiering. He had reached the elevated rank of general the hard way. Born in Stobs in Roxburghshire, the youngest son of a Scottish laird whose sympathies, if the names George Augustus are anything to go by, were with the new Hanoverian dynasty, he was sent to Holland to extend his education at the renowned university in Leyden. George Eliott took the business of becoming a soldier far more seriously than was common at that time, as he followed up the Leyden education with a spell at a French military academy and a course of instruction as a field engineer in Woolwich.

This combination of natural talent and specialist training should have placed him head and shoulders above the English gentlemen who provided the British regiment with their officers. It would be more truthful to say that it enabled him to offset the absence of funds or family connections which provided at that time the entrée to the officer class. He also did something about those deficiencies, marrying a wealthy Devonshire heiress descended from Sir Francis Drake. By 1754, he had reached the rank of lieutenant-colonel, and had become a strict disciplinarian, a teetotaller and vegetarian, preoccupied with health, fitness and exercise, an asset to any army but a mixed blessing to the men who served under him.

His army career bristled with action. He fought at Dettingen in 1743 (that battle at which the British were victorious but which is known chiefly to quiz-addicts as the last time a British monarch commanded an army in the field) and at Fontenoy in 1744 (this time on the losing side under the Duke of Cumberland). It would seem likely that he rushed back home with his general to fight for Hanoverian against Jacobite at the Battle of Culloden. George II took a very special liking to the talented Scot who had fought with him at Dettingen—and asked him to set up Britain's first new-style mobile unit on the pattern of the Prussian hussars.

He was back in Europe for a valiant contribution to the German campaign of 1759-1761 and then crossed the Atlantic to fight in Cuba. This time military success was accompanied by a welcome accumulation of £25,000 prize money for his part in the capture of Havana—a sum that enabled him to buy the estate of Heathfield in Sussex.

With such a full military career behind him, General Eliott could hardly have expected his next appointment—in 1777 he was put in command of the fortress of Gibraltar on that bold, rocky tear that drops from the tip of Spain. He was horrified at what he found there. Captured from the Spanish by Sir George Rooke in 1704, the Rock had at first been seen as a vital acquisition to the British naval presence, but almost immediately it lost out to the new naval base of Port Mahon in the Balearics. By the time General Eliott came to take charge it was, far from being a key strategic stronghold, a dilapidated vulnerable corner of the British Empire. In the bay, a single man-o-war, three frigates and a sloop formed the total British muster. The defences were crumbling, the garrison reduced to a dangerous level and provisions totally inadequate for a siege.

To a man like Eliott this neglect bordered on the criminal. He subjected London to a bombardment of requests to try and repair the ravages but when on 11 July 1779 Spain launched an attack on the fortress, the garrison numbered fewer than 6000 men. In the early build-up to the attack Eliott had offered civilians free passages out of Gibraltar.

Eliott's professionalism could hardly have been applied in a more crucial situation. He had prepared for the siege meticulously, digging up street surfaces using teams of eighty men pulling ploughs to reduce richochets, removing all unnecessary towers including church spires. His thoroughness was awesome.

The siege was to last three years and seven months, an impregnable Rock defended by vulnerable soldiers who needed food and ammunition. These could only be provided by the Royal Navy, extended by the demands of the American War of Independence and even having to contend with the depredations of John Paul Jones nearer home.

Eliott masterminded the defences impressively—and the navy relieved the defenders at three crucial times in the siege. The defenders could have had any of a legion of effete and ineffective British officers in command; they had Eliott. Food? The General, to show just what could be done, lived on four ounces of rice a day for over a week and even prevented his officers from using flour on their hair—a practice which the British army did not abandon until 1808. Boredom? He personally led a daring sortie to spike the twenty-eight enemy guns and blow up magazine and stores. Surprise attack? He introduced the invading Floating Batteries to the new idea of red-hot cannon-balls. Shortages in manpower? He armed the musicians, to the annoyance of officers who regarded them as personal cabaret.

At the end of forty-three months, the farrago of mercenaries from Savoy and Naples, Flanders and France, Ireland and Malta, abandoned both the siege and the Spanish flag and went home, leaving the Rock very much the heavier from all the cannon-balls it had absorbed (on 12 July 1781 for example 150,000 balls and 60,000 thirteen-inch shells had thudded into the fortress)—but undeniably British.

Sieges rarely capture the imagination of the public or the military historians, rivalling Continental Drift as the most soporific of study topics. This one did. The superlative General Eliott was honoured with a peerage in 1787, becoming Lord Heathfield of Gibraltar. In 1967, a century and a half after his birth, Gibraltar remembered him with a fine set of postage stamps. The 2s stamp shows Eliott commanding defence operations, while the 9d shows the Heathfield tower and monument in Sussex.

John Paul Jones
1747-1792

I have not yet begun to fight

John Paul Jones
US Bicentennial 15c

—the patriot they called pirate

In the early summer of 1905, four United States cruisers, *Brooklyn*, *Tacoma*, *Chattanooga* and *Galveston*, crossed the Atlantic to France on a very special mission—to bring back for

President Theodore Roosevelt the body of a Scot who had been buried outside the walls of Paris more than a century before. That Scot was John Paul Jones, charismatic swashbuckler and the most colourful fighting sailor to be produced by the American War of Independence.

Little about the man was ordinary; even his name was an amalgam of two—John Paul, the name he was born with and John Jones, the one he assumed to wriggle out of a lynching in Tobago.

John Paul was born on 6 July 1747 on the estate of Arbigland in the parish of Kirkbean, son of the estate gardener John Paul and his wife Jean Macduff. The middle child of a family of seven, he grew up in the tidy, comfortable cottage which still exists today as the home of one of the estate workers. From this house, on all but the greyest day, the freckled, sandy-haired lad could see the opposing coast of England and between the two countries the Solway Firth, busy with sea trade. With the lure of the doorstep sea so strong, the youngster at the age of thirteen crossed the Firth to the port of Whitehaven, signed on as an apprentice and set off on the Barbados-Virginia run.

John Paul quickly learnt the skills of handling a ship and the business dealings that went with it, and lost no time in laying down the foundations of his reputation as a fiery and demanding character, feared by men and favoured by women.

When fever swept through one of the vessels he was working on, it killed off the master and his mate and left young Paul in command of ship. He handled the surprise responsibilities so well that the grateful owners gave him a permanent command—a master at the age of twenty-one without benefit of family influence.

The short, dapper, wiry Scot was a stickler for discipline and this led him into a number of scrapes, culminating in an incident in Tobago where he killed the ringleader of a grumbling mutiny. Chances of a fair trial seemed remote and John Paul slipped away, using the name of John Jones, perhaps to take over a vessel from a captain of that name.

The runaway went to earth for a couple of years on the mainland of America. There his skills as a seaman were at a premium, with the conflict in North America building up to a direct confrontation between Britain and her colonies. On 7 December 1775, John Paul Jones (the 'Paul' may have been restored to distinguish himself from the many John Jones among the Welshmen of Pennsylvania) was appointed a first lieutenant in the Continental Navy. He took part in some of the early skirmishes between the British merchant and naval vessels and the ragbag of ships and crews that served as a navy for the colonists. Jones believed, however, that the real role of any navy formed by the colonists was not to meet the British warships head-on, but to go and seek out the weak spots of the Royal Navy and strike there. In June 1777, he was appointed Captain of the *Ranger* and set off on a daring demonstration of his theory—a direct assault on Britain itself and an attack on a British town.

Sailing up between Ireland and Great Britain, Jones took and sunk the brigantine *Dolphin* and captured the 250-ton *Lord Chattan* of Dublin. As he approached what was for him home territory, he decided on a bold stroke: to raid the port of Whitehaven from which he had sailed as a ship's boy in 1760 and put out of action the colliers and fishing boats there. His crew were almost in mutiny: there was no pickings to be had in sinking such small fry. But Jones, mindful of the publicity value and knowing the British mentality better than his New England crew, carried it through, a botched, half-hearted affair which nevertheless threw Britain into turmoil and, as the Commander was recognised by some of the locals, brought the name of John Paul Jones into the headlines. The last raid on an English port had been by the Dutch in 1667. Where was the Royal Navy?

Disappointed with the results of the raid (he was not able to see the newspapers!), Jones decided on an alternative strategem: he would sail across to Scotland and kidnap the Earl of Selkirk. With such an important person in his grasp (the mature Commander was perhaps relying on childhood memories in gauging the Earl's significance to the British Government!), he could demand the release of the colonial sailors being kept in British prisons. In common with many other Americans, Jones was furious at the practice of treating colonial seamen as pirates and not as combatants.

A small party of men, led by Jones, landed and made their way to the Earl's home. He was out when they called, but the men wanted something to show for their venture—the family silver would do nicely. Jones agreed they should do this but insisted that they must behave like gentlemen (not, from the evidence of North American campaigns, like Englishmen). The men delivered a note to the Countess giving the assurance of Commodore John Paul Jones that, if the family silver was handed over, no person and no other property would be touched. The Countess was aloof and dignified. She scolded the butler for trying to hide some of the silver, arranged for the party to borrow sacks and even asked for a receipt. The men took the silver back to their waiting commander. When he heard of the Countess' handling of the situation he was so impressed that when the silver came up for auction back in France, he bought it himself and wrote a letter to the Countess promising to return it when hostilities were over. Despite a frosty reply from the Earl, Jones was true to that promise.

Jones prepared to leave Britain, but the *Ranger* mission was not to end with the Selkirk anticlimax. Leaving the Solway, Jones spotted *HMS Drake* and before crowds of watchers on the Ulster coast won an hour-long battle, capturing 133 officers and men of His Britannic Majesty's Navy.

If *Ranger* was a success, however, Jones' next operation was a triumph. Taking command of a new ship, a wallowing, sluggish East Indiaman renamed *Bonhomme Richard,* he assembled a motley squadron of unreliable privateers and no less unreliable naval vessels and sailed round the west coast of Ireland, north between Orkney and Shetland and down the east coast of Scotland, capturing small merchant ships as he went. Having failed to bring off a dazzling raid on the Solway, he determined to rectify matters in the Forth, capturing not a country aristocrat but the port of Leith, on the very threshold of Scotland's capital.

The approach of Jones' squadron sent the east coast into panic stations. The country's militia had been disbanded as a precautionary measure after the Jacobite scare of 1745. Defence of the coast had been ignored for decades, but now people could think of little else. Sir John Anstruther of Elie on the north bank of the Forth felt moved to look for some gunpowder to convert his ceremonial brass cannon into something more useful and despatched a servant in a boat to borrow some from *HMS Romney*. The servant boarded the warship, delivered his letter and was given a hundredweight of powder. As it was being stowed aboard his boat, he told the captain the news of "that rebel John Paul Jones, a pirate who ought to be hanged." The captain took ill-concealed delight in telling the poor fellow that he was on the wrong ship and addressing not Captain Johnston of the *Romney*, but the very pirate for whom he had such unpleasant proposals. Edinburgh and Leith were quaking, but a strong gale-force wind drove Jones' squadron down the Forth and saved the day for the Scots.

Jones set off southwards, his vessels trailing an impressive string of captured merchant ships behind them. On the way to Newcastle to cut off London's winter coal supply, Jones lobbed a playful cannonball into the garden of Bamburgh Castle and proceeded as far as Scarborough. There the squadron sighted forty-one vessels on the horizon, a rich convoy from the Baltic, shepherded by the frigate *Serapis* (fifty guns) and the sloop-o-war *Countess of Scarborough*. To get at the merchantmen, Jones would have to deal with the warships first. *Bonhomme Richard* took on the faster, more manoeuvrable, more powerfully armed *Serapis*. It was to be Jones' greatest challenge and his greatest victory.

Early in the confrontation, *Serapis* asked Jones if he had

struck (lowered his flag as a sign of surrender) and Jones replied in the words which feature on many of the stamps which commemorate him "I have not yet begun to fight." He proceeded to show that this was no idle piece of bravado. He eventually got to grips with the *Serapis*, the only tactic which stood any chance of success. In the clinch the *Serapis* could not risk a broadside into *Bonhomme Richard*. Jones stayed there in a long and bloody encounter, watched by swarms of onlookers on Flamborough Head.

Bonhomme Richard emerged at the end of the carnage as victor, thanks to the muskets and handgrenades which slowly disposed of *Serapis'* crew. No-one looking at the combatants at the end of the battle could have possibly believed that the American vessel had won. It was on the point of disintegrating when the British captain Pearson "struck," surrendering to what Samuel Eliot Morison in his excellent life of Jones described as "little more than a battered raft."

The glory in the most spectacular one-to-one battle to be fought in British waters marked the end of Jones' short and flamboyant contribution to the War of American Independence. Handicapped always by unsuitable ships, mixed and hostile crews, surly and even mutinous officers, John Paul Jones showed the new nation of the United States the need for a navy and for the audacity to go with it. The remaining thirteen years of his life were a sad reward. The French King decorated him—and indeed it is in the dress of a Chevalier of France that he appears on the stamp issued in 1980 by the USA—but he was never during his lifetime adequately recognised or adequately used by the nation he served so well. Eventually he was appointed to be US Consul in Algiers. Before the news reached him he had died a poor man in Paris, having wasted his final years in fruitless naval duties in the Black Sea fighting for Catherine the Great of Russia. The US Consul in Paris had been unable to attend his funeral as he was getting ready for a dinner party.

The United States came to acknowledge Jones' value and to

acknowledge it handsomely, in a number of ways. One of these was the search for Jones' body and its return to the USA—the mission of those four cruisers in 1905. Fifty years later a single vessel, *USS Paul Jones*, made a similar transatlantic voyage, this time carrying a plaque from the Naval Historical Foundation and the Army and Navy Chapter of the Daughters of the American Revolution to adorn the wall of the small cottage on the Arbigland estate where John Paul was born.

Thomas Cochrane 1775-1860

—Scotland's greatest seaman

As 1813 turned into 1814, the people of Europe were aware that yet another year had passed by with the nations locked in the seemingly endless Napoleonic Wars.

For Britain, the first sign of an end came in the middle of night of 20-21 February when a uniformed French officer, Lieutenant Colonel du Bourg, came ashore at Dover, called for speedy transport to London and a messenger to take urgent news to the post at Deal. No-one was left in doubt as to the news he brought: the French had been defeated and Napoleon killed.

By the time the Frenchman reached the City, the place was agog with the news which ran like bushfire ahead of him. The price of Government stock rose optimistically at the news of a clean and final peace.

There was, alas, no "Lieutenant Colonel du Bourg" and no truth whatsoever in the story. The whole plot had been hatched to make fools of the city financiers and millionaires of a few crooks. In the angry post-mortem which followed, the culprits were tracked down and with them an undoubted innocent, Lord Thomas Cochrane. It was a tragedy from which Cochrane, the only man to challenge Nelson for the honour of being Britain's greatest seamen, never recovered. He was savagely sentenced to a fine of £1000, to a year in prison and to stand in the pillory for an hour. Cochrane had won so many enemies with his naval exploits and his political attacks that these were not the only punishments. He was removed without hesitation from the Navy List, and his banners pulled down from among those of his fellow peers in the Order of the Bath.

His naval career in tatters as far as the Royal Navy was concerened, in 1817 he accepted an invitation to go and command the fleet of Chile in the nation's quest for independence from the Spanish crown. It was the start of a new career which was to win him the fame and honour which had been denied him at home.

The Chileans were undoubtedly getting the most daring, talented and innovative sailor in the world. Born in Annfield, Lanarkshire, Thomas Cochrane was brought up at Culross Abbey, the family's mouldering seat on the Fife shore. His father was the ninth Earl of Dundonald, a man brimming with creativity (he was the inventor of coal-gas lighting) but devoid of business acumen (he used the coal-gas lighting only to amuse some party guests and then went off on some other tack). The combination frequently produces poverty, and it did so in this case.

Young Thomas Cochrane joined the navy at the age of seventeen and rapidly established himself as a man to be reckoned with. He commanded his first vessel in 1800, a small brig *Speedy*, equipped with almost negligible fire power. Nevertheless Cochrane managed in thirteen months to capture more than fifty vessels and 500 prisoners. The methods he used to chalk up such figures were imaginative and brave. Napoleon referred with grudging admiration to "Le Loup de Mer," the Sea Wolf.

The Admiralty were unimpressed, haggling over promotion

with such strange logic that although Cochrane had performed an astonishing feat, the number of men lost in the action was not considered great enough to justify a suitable reward! Cochrane, the scourge of Mediterranean shipping, was promoted to the command of a leaky collier, protecting the fisheries around Shetland.

By the end of 1804, new faces at the Admiralty removed Cochrane from his heel-kicking in the north and gave him the *Pallas,* a newly-launched frigate. Again, Cochrane broke all records capturing rich Spanish and French ships at will, including some £75,000 of prize money in three days as his own share. Later promotion to the *Impérieuse* continued Cochrane's relentless success. It culminated in a brilliant achievement: cracking the shell which protected the French fleet anchored at the island of Aix. "You may quiet your apprehensions that the enemy will attempt something against the isle of Aix," Napoleon had written, "nothing can be more insane than the idea of attacking a French squadron [there]." He was forgetting the fertile brain of the Sea Wolf.

Cochrane was delegated over the heads of senior commanders to find a way into the protected area. He prepared his secret weapon as the fire-ships were assembled. Three transport vessels were specially strengthened to resist the explosion of the barrels of gunpowder and channel the force directly into the great boom which protected the French squadron. Six miles away the British ships under Admiral Gambier lay at anchor, ready to follow up Cochrane's breach operation.

The French admiral saw the fire-ships approach and took all the precautions he felt necessary, although he could not see how fire-ships could break the boom. He did not know about Cochrane's exploding ships, the devastating new floating mines.

Cochrane's plan went off to perfection. The first "mine," with Cochrane aboard, reached the boom. Cochrane and his men lit the fuses and retired in a boat. The vessel exploded with a terrifying roar, closely followed by the second "mine." The impregnable boom was well and truly breached and in through the gap sailed the fire-ships. The French fleet was in complete disarray as terror swept through the crews. They were not to know that the fire-ships would not produce the same devastation as the explosive-ships. Ships collided in panic. Water was thrown on the gunpowder to prevent explosions on the French vessels. Many were grounded in the confusion.

As dawn broke, Cochrane delivered to his admiral the plumpest sitting duck in the history of the British Navy. All the French ships were seriously damaged, all but two grounded. The firepower of the French was drastically reduced by the protective action of soaking the gunpowder. Admiral Gambier held back, ignoring messages of despair from Cochrane. Eventually the Scot took his own frigate in to the midst of the French fleet and set to work. Gambier eventually, eight hours late, sent in a single man-o-war to help Cochrane, but kept the rest of his fleet six miles away. After wreaking all the destruction he could, Cochrane was forced to withdraw as the great French war-ships were released by the tide from their stranded position on the beach. Gambier had fluffed the kill.

In the inevitable court martial, Gambier's well-placed friends came to his rescue and he emerged with a knighthood and a pat on the back from the Government. The hero of the hour, Cochrane, was furious—and not even his own accolade of Knight of the Order of the Bath could dampen his anger. It was, although he could not have known it at the time, the last chance he would have to fight at sea for Britain.

This then was the man who, ignored by the Admiralty and framed in the financial fraud, sailed into Valparaiso Bay on 28 November 1818. His timing was superb. As Ian Grimble describes in his magnificient biography *The Sea Wolf*, "The Admiral of Chile invited his new colleagues to a dinner on St Andrew's Night. Great was the astonishment and admiration when this tall and imposing man presided at it in the full dress of a Highland Chief."

Despite infighting and intrigue which would have done justice to the British Admiralty, Cochrane's work to win the sea battles which were essential to consolidate the land victories already achieved by the Chileans was spectacularly successful, accomplished with his usual blend of the unpredictable and the courageous. He captured Valdivia, "the Gibraltar of the Pacific" and the Spanish were on the retreat. Chile was free and Cochrane moved north to perform the same service for Peru. He did it in true Cochrane style. Convinced as ever that surprise was the greatest element in any victory he reasoned that what would surprise the Spanish more than anything else would be to be attacked by just one ship. He did just that, striking at night and carrying off the Spanish flagship *Esmeralda*—a coup that was, ironically, watched and admired by Captain Sir Thomas Hardy, the man who has entered history as the companion of that other great British sailor, Horatio Nelson. Hardy was in command of the Royal Navy's South America Squadron anchored in Quito harbour.

The tales of Cochrane's epic deeds spread throughout the world and he was in demand. He went on to command the Brazilian navy in its struggle against the Portuguese—at one stage pursuing the entire Portuguese fleet across the Atlantic with only one vessel of his own. (At the end of that pursuit, he had the flag of the new republic saluted at Portsmouth—its first acknowledgment—in the same way as his fellow Scot, John Paul Jones, had had the Stars and Stripes given its first international recognition by the French.)

After similar exploits in Greece, he eventually won the long battle to have his name restored at home and returned to Britain. On 2 May 1832, the Royal pardon was recorded and a week later the naval hero of four nations attended a Royal levée as rear Admiral Dundonald (he had inherited his father's title as 10th Earl of Dundonald).

The Sea Wolf settled down to many remaining years in Britain, dying in 1860 at the ripe age of 85. There has not been space to talk of his brilliant inventive streak inherited (with little else) from his father and applied to a range of problems not just naval but also including general engineering (he helped out Brunel with an invention to control air pressures in tunnelling, his patent being first used in the USA's Hudson Tunnel). There has likewise been no space to talk about his political career as a radical, red-tape-hitting MP—but his honours at home have been slight. Fighting vessels in the fleets of the nations he liberated have been named after him; in Britain a shore-base in Scotland is the only operation to bear it. Indeed, when Britain, to aid the war effort in 1917, took over a vessel built in Britain for the Chilean Navy, she changed its name from *Admiral Cochrane* (the name chosen by Chile) to *HMS Eagle*.

The Sea Wolf's talents were wasted by the gap between his brilliance and his inability to compromise with his superiors. In the prologue to his finest play, George Bernard Shaw, comparing the lives of three martyrs, declared: "It is always difficult for superior spirits to contemplate the fury aroused by their exposure of comparative dullards." Despite the spell studying philosophy at Edinburgh during one of his frequent "fallow" spells with the British Admiralty, Cochrane would have smiled at any comparison with Socrates and Jesus. He would surely have found something in common, however, with the third—St Joan—another military leader who suffered more from her own side than from the enemy.

Arthur J. Balfour 1848-1930

—foppish politician, toast of the Jews

On 19 March 1930, the A'skara, the Jewish Prayer of Remembrance, was chanted in synagogues in honour of a most unlikely hero, an effete, foppish British politician of extremely right wing views, a dilettante millionaire with more than a touch of the antisemitism which tinged the British upper classes at the turn of the century.

There was nothing in Arthur James Balfour's background to suggest the bold Zionist pronouncement which was to win him the gratitude of world Jewry and a spot on an Israeli postage stamp. He was born on the beautiful estate of Whittinghame in East Lothian, his father wealthy heir to a fortune amassed in India, his mother coming from one of England's oldest and most prominent families, a Cecil and sister to the Marquis of Salisbury.

He progressed, as a good Tory should, to Eton and then to Trinity College, Cambridge. He got a speedy entry into the world's most exclusive club, the House of Commons, via a safe family seat in Hertford and the good offices of his uncle, Lord Salisbury. He did not show any spark to suggest a future leader. Indeed for two years he remained silent on the benches. He broke his silence during a debate on Indian currency with what he described as a "dull speech on a dull subject delivered to an empty house by an anxious beginner." He retired into his shell for another year and acquired the reputation of "at best as a parliamentary *flâneur*, a trifler with debate."

In his uncle's administrations he was given a few minor posts until in 1887, when Lord Salisbury appointed his nephew to the sharp-end post of Chief Secretary for Ireland, then as now a rather dangerous promotion. (The phrase "Bob's your uncle" came into a vogue at about this time, although opinion is divided as to whether or not A. J. Balfour and his uncle Robert were at the root of it.)

When Salisbury resigned in 1902, Balfour became Prime Minister and ran Britain with more skill than his pince-nez and golfing outings, langour and cynicism, might suggest. Despite his Scottishness, he contrived to portray what the rest of the world wanted an aristocratic English milord to look like—and no-one since, not even fellow Scot Sir Alec Douglas Home, has ever managed to beat him at it.

In the year in which Balfour ended his term as Prime Minister, he met Chaim Weizman and was introduced to the concept of the Zionist state. The idea appealed to him "It is not a dream; it is a great cause and I understand it." Balfour came back on to the centre-stage of politics when he was drafted into the War Cabinet as an elder statesman. In that capacity, with the war still in progress but with Britain looking already to the post-war politics, Balfour drafted and got the Government to issue the following statement: "His Majesty's Government view with favour the establishment in Palestine of a national home for the Jewish people and will use their best endeavours to facilitate the achievement of this object, it being clearly understood that nothing shall be done which may prejudice the civil and religious rights of existing non-Jewish communities in Palestine or the rights and political status enjoyed by Jews in any other country."

It was many years before the prodigious putting back of the clock nearly two thousand years took place. And when the Jews did return to the Promised Land, the first settlement was called Balfouria. Arthur James Balfour did not live long enough to see the state of Israel, as he died in 1930 and was buried on the family estate of Whittinghame.

Allan Wilson
1856-1893

—White Rhodesia's
General Custer

The British have puzzled other nations with their ecstatic worship of the gallant loser—sometimes, it seems, at the expense of the gallant winner. Although the trait is most firmly established in the Anglo-Saxon corner of the kingdom, the leading names in British mythology—Gordon of Khartoum and Scott of the Antarctic—have a distinctly Scottish ring about them. The only native-born Scot to feature as a gallant loser on a postage stamp is Major Allan Wilson, the General Custer of White Rhodesia.

Wilson gained his painful fame in the Matabele War, which at the end of 1892 was dragging on inconclusively, with the native king Lobengula still alive and struggling. The British were convinced that until Lobengula was captured or killed there could be no clean end to the war. Unknown to them, the king was already suing for peace, having sent one of his commanders with a note to that effect and 1000 gold sovereigns to seek out the British forces. The man was captured and the bag of gold, far from ensuring that the message would be delivered, tempted his captors, two British troopers, to run off with the sovereigns and ignore the more important piece of paper.

In appalling weather, Major Allan Wilson, born at White Bog, near the hamlet of Glenurquhart on the Black Isle, and educated in Orkney and at Fochabers, decided to cross the Shangani river in pursuit of Lobengula, taking with him fifteen men. Beleiving he was closing in on the king, he sent back across the river for reinforcements and was joined with a small support force of 21 men before the river's surge cut him off from the main party. Wilson and 36 troopers disappeared from the sight of the main force. Gunfiring was heard from the direction in which Wilson had marched but it was not for another two months after the death of Lobengula and the end of the war that the story of the soldiers came to light. Wilson and his soldiers were surrounded by Lobengula's warriors. They fought in true Victorian style to the last bullet, and then sang the national anthem as they were wiped out with club, assegai and bullet.

The bodies were burried at nearby Zimbabwe, a spot later to give its name to the black successor to Rhodesia, but were removed to a spot alongside Rhodes and Jamieson and the other makers of the nation. A massive monument marks the spot and the scene of Wilson's stand adorned many a public building in Rhodesia.

James Connolly
1868-1916

—the Irish martyr from Edinburgh

On 12 May 1916, in the retribution and aftermath of the Easter Uprising in Dublin against the British Government, the last of the ringleaders to be shot died before a firing squad, sitting in a chair. He was James Connolly, unable to stand because of a bullet wound in the ankle received during his defence of the General Post Office building in O'Connell Street.

It may seem out of keeping to include in this book a man viewed by himself, his followers and his enemies as an Irishman. Connolly was, however, born in Edinburgh. That point is of more than academic interest, because while his Irish parents determined *where* he was to fight his battle, his Scottish upbringing had an important rôle to play in moulding the pattern of his fight. He was to carry to Dublin the socialism and republicanism of the Scottish proletariat.

He was born on 5 June 1868, son of a Monaghan couple who had left Ireland to escape the poverty of the land and finished up with John Connolly toiling as a manure carter in one of Edinburgh's most run-down quarters. The deprivation in which the family was brought up was extreme. Not even Dublin could have offered more abject living conditions; the Irish Capital could certainly not provide the tradition of radical political thought which was seething in Scotland at that time. The exposure to this "attitude" and the links which Connolly was to have with the socialist movement in Scotland throughout his political life made a powerful contribution to the development of the struggle for independence in Ireland.

At fourteen, Connolly took one of the attractive ways out of his appalling environment. He joined the army. The military life was not for him and he fled from Ireland, where he was posted, back to Scotland.

When he returned to Ireland it was with a very clear, single-minded aim: to organise the working people into a cohesive political force. He saw trade unionism as the way of achieving this. By the turn of the century, he, along with the abrasive Jim Larkin (significantly a product like Connolly of Irish parents and mainland proletariat, in his case Liverpool) had organised the Irish Transport Union and were holding out against management. They provided the Irish with a positive example of how a militant trade union could carry the struggle to the powerful owners of Dublin's tramways.

Connolly's "Scottish" socialism was soon wedded to an "Irish" nationalism when he realised that his goal could be best achieved in an independent, republican Ireland. The outbreak of the European War in 1914 concentrated London's attentions elsewhere and revived the old Fenian adage of "England's difficulty was Ireland's opportunity." Connolly was as eager as any to attack.

He had built up alongside his Irish Transport Union

activities the Irish Citizen Army, armed and uniformed, which paraded openly outside the Union headquarters at Liberty Hall and boasted a paramilitary presence which in the context of present-day Ulster seems acceptable enough but which was almost unthinkable in 1916 in the heart of one of the Empire's main cities.

Plans were made for an uprising on Easter Monday, with arms and the significant presence of Sir Roger Casement guaranteed by a German submarine. The British Government was alerted and moved with impressive timing to quash the danger. Casement was captured as he landed and the vessel carrying the arms was scuttled. Connolly and the other leaders were to be arrested, but as the Monday was a Bank Holiday and the crowds would be keen to get to the racing at Fairyhouse, orders to disarm the paramilitaries and arrest the leaders were postponed until the Tuesday. On Monday, the rebels struck.

From a military point of view, the Uprising was doomed. The rebels took control of the large and impressive Post Office in the heart of the city, but the British sealed off and surrounded the area and slowly bombarded the building into submission. The populace had not leapt to the aid of the minority freedom fighters and indeed, as many of the Dubliners had friends and relatives fighting the Germans in the trenches of Europe, the rebels were subjected to a fair amount of abuse. The leaders surrendered, and Connolly was carried from the Post Office on a stretcher with gangrene developing in an ankle wound. The British authorities started on court martial procedures and executions, and the mood of the Dubliners changed. Connolly and his colleagues, military failures, became nationalist martyrs and the bold aggresive socialist from Edinburgh had made a telling, posthumous contribution to the independence of Ireland, but little, as subsequent events have shown, to the cause which was closer to his heart, the emancipation of the working classes.

John Maclean 1879-1923

—convict 2652 and Soviet Consul in Glasgow

After the successful Bolshevik Revolution of 1917, the first Congress of Soviets in Petrograd elected as honorary presidents Lenin, Trotsky and a Glasgow school-teacher in his late thirties by the name of John Maclean. Within the year, the Scot had been further honoured, this time by Lenin, as the first Bolshevik Consul for Scotland. The office was to prove more honorary than onerous as the British Post Office refused to acknowledge the Consul's existence and returned all mail sent to him by his Ambassador in London. HM Customs hardly helped matters by confiscating the cheque for £5000 sent from Moscow to pay for the running of the Glasgow office.

As we have seen from the other Scots in this section, freedom fighters only become famous if they are on the winning side, whether immediately or ultimately. John Maclean, a household name in his day, was honoured on a Soviet postage stamp in 1979, but by then had become virtually unknown not only in Britain at large but also in his native Scotland. Maclean was a freedom fighter on the losing side.

If it was ever possible to read a man's future from his past, it could have been done in the case of John Maclean. On both sides of his family, his roots lay in the harsh crofting communities of the Highlands and Islands, although his forebears were torn out of their communities and transplanted into the industrialised central belt of Scotland. His father was a potter, dying from a respiratory disease when John was only eight. His mother was a weaver and a shopkeeper. His family had been evicted by landed interests and exploited by industrial ones.

Throughout this book, many stories tell of the education of a poor child at great sacrifice on the part of his family. In John Maclean's case, this was again true, with his mother struggling to send John and his brother Daniel to the University of Glasgow.

Writing of his early life, Maclean declared: "It was the knowledge of the sacrifices made and the self-denial endured by my mother and sisters to enable me to be educated that made me resolve to use my education in the service of the workers."

Maclean's comment shows a distinct variation on other stories of educated poor boys, and perhaps even a change of direction from the aims that his family had in mind when making those sacrifices. Maclean saw education not as a magic key that would allow him to unlock his personal shackles and fly from the working class, but as a "skeleton" key which he could use to unlock the shackles of the entire working class.

He qualified as a teacher, but his real contribution to "education" came outside the classroom. He believed that education was at the heart of any progress towards socialism, that ignorance was the strongest of the links in the chain that held the workers in thrall to capitalism. He set about to banish that ignorance, through meetings, letters, debates, articles and his own evening classes. A study of the principles of economics—naturally Marxian economics—would, he believed, persuade the workers that the status quo was neither inevitable nor eternal—and give them the means of bringing it to an end.

When war broke out in 1914, Maclean had no doubts. This was not a war of national interests; it was a war about capitalist interests. It was not until the next war that the slogan emerged "A bayonet is a weapon with a worker at each end," but it sums up Maclean's attitude to the Balkan conflict which sucked in the whole of Europe. Maclean's pacifism infuriated a Government fighting a desperate war and in 1915 Maclean was fined £5 for his utterances under the Defence of the Realm

K

Act. He opted for the prison sentence and was sacked from his job. A year later he was in greater trouble, sentenced to hard labour for open sedition. The same offence brought him into court again in May 1918, accused of seditious public speeches in the west of Scotland.

In particular, Maclean was accused of prejudicing the recruiting, discipline and the administration of His Majesty's Forces. Not even a spectacular and impassioned defence by Maclean could save him and he was sentenced to five years' penal servitude. He left prison physically broken, but continued to pursue his campaign relentlessly, continuing his barrage of pamphlets, speeches and debates.

His final political speech was delivered on a foggy Glasgow night in November 1923. A few days later, pneumonia struck dead Scotland's mildest and most pacifist freedom fighter.

SCOTS— ROYAL & LORDLY

James VI and I
1566-1625

—the King who became King

On 24 March 1603, Queen Elizabeth of England died, aged 69, and the Tudors, fertile in talent if not in heirs, were finished. The line of succession now ran back through the years to the wily Welsh founder of the dynasty, Henry Tudor, and then via his daughter Margaret who had married the King of Scotland, down the line of Scottish monarchs to the current incumbent, James VI. Sir Robert Carey jumped on his horse and galloped north on a sixty-hour journey to Edinburgh to tell James VI that he was now James I of England as well. The news did not come as a shock to James; his spies in London had kept him fully posted on the health of his great-aunt Elizabeth.

James left Scotland, with more than a little relief, to take up the new office south of the Border. His experiences in Scotland had not been happy ones. Born in Edinburgh Castle on 19 June 1566, he had succeeded to the throne before his second birthday as the only son of Mary, Queen of Scots. His mother had been forced to give up her throne by powerful pressure groups.

James's youthful reign was a bloody one, with successive regents being murdered and replaced by rival nobles. Even when he did come to take over personal control he was immediately put under "protective custody" by yet another power group. When he eventually escaped from this influence he fought a fairly successful resistance against others who wanted to do his ruling for him.

Over this tumultuous period James, rather like an oyster throwing a pearly protection around a piece of grit, was developing his concept of the Divine Right of Kings, a belief that monarchs derived their power from God and it was not to be circumscribed by Church or Parliament. He was not getting very far with the practice of this Right in Scotland—he must have felt that he stood a better chance in England.

Unfortunately, he was not built for his task. Whether one is preaching the Divine Right of Kings or the Theory of the Master Race, it does help to look the part. James was a poor physical specimen, timid, disfigured by his stab-proof padding (a legacy of his Regent days of insecurity), hesitant and even incomprehensible in speech. He refused to believe that the opposition to his ideas expressed by the English Parliament represented a genuine and widely held political opinion. He was convinced that it was the work of "some few vipers." He even went so far as to tear out of the Journals of the House a declaration setting out to state the rights and privileges of Englishmen.

His autocratic approach, his favourites, his contempt for Parliament, built up a resentment of the monarchy that ensured that his son and successor, Charles I, would have a rough and unruly reception when he began, with greater talent and determination, to apply his father's principles.

James makes the postage stamps in his role as the founder of British influence in Newfoundland. It was one of many very positive benefits which came in his reign but which tend to get overpowered by his image as "The Wisest Fool in Christendom" and "God's Sillie Vassal." But anyone who gave golf to the English, the Authorised Version of the Bible to the world, the lobelia to gardeners and, via a dowry from Anne of Denmark, the oil-rich seas around Orkney and Shetland to the UK economy deserves a little bit more consideration than those nicknames suggest.

Charles I
1600-1649

—the King who lost his head

It is no easy task for a British monarch to win a lasting place in the consciousness of his or her subjects. The monarch needs to acquire something very special such as an encounter with a spider in a cave, a penchant for burning cakes, a hump-back, six wives or rumours of virginity. Some never made the grade even when seeming to have a very distinctive start: George I spoke only German and not even that was enough.

Charles I seemed to have a chance early on. He was playing a round of "gowff" on his favourite links at Leith when a galloping messenger brought the news that the Irish were rebelling. He insisted on finishing his round. So far so good— he seemed likely to outdo Sir Francis Drake. But whereas Sir Francis had finished his game of bowls and then gone off to cuff the Diegos in their armada, Charles completed his round of gowff and went and lost to the Irish, the Scots and the English in turn. Tragically he had a second chance to gain his fame; he was executed by the command of Parliament.

How did Charles get into the situation? He was born at Dunfermline, ancient seat of Scottish kings, on 19 November 1625, the last Scottish monarch to be born in Scotland. He was, however, brought up in England and was the first ruler to be raised in the Church of England. He developed a deep and fatal love for the church and its beliefs and rituals. To this basic loyalty were added two strands which were scarcely less dangerous in seventeenth-century Britain: Charles inherited his father's concept of the Divine Right of a monarch and married a French princess who believed that her husband in Britain should rule as her father in France had done.

The fatal combination brought Charles into quick and

intense confrontation with a House of Commons, that was Puritan in sympathies and conscious of its own rights and responsibilities. Charles' pressing need was cash—and the only way to get it was to call Parliament and get permission to levy taxes. But the Parliament members knew the strength of their position and wanted Charles to settle a few accumulated grievances before letting him loose on the tax-payers of England. He dismissed the Parliament and when he came to call a second excluded difficult members. It did not work and again he had to dissolve the Parliament without getting the money he wanted. By the time Parliament came up for third round it was seething at the attempts to bring in a new-style religion with more than a few echoes of Rome, and almost apoplectic at Charles' attempts to raise money by non-Parliamentary means. It passed legislation to give these grievances teeth, even resorting to holding down the Speaker of the House, who was a king's man but whose presence was necessary to the passing of any laws.

Charles in a controlled rage dismissed Parliament and in an effort to show who was boss ruled for eleven years without it. In order to levy cash he came up with a series of devices which taxed the ingenuity of his advisers and countless generations of British schoolchildren. One will perhaps give the flavour of his arbitary approach to fund-raising. In the dim and distant past, ports had paid ship-money, a sort of collective insurance to help man the boats and drive off pirates. Charles, in the absence of any significant build-up of pirates in the English Channel, revived the levy—and not content with that extended it to inland rural villages. Farmers who had never ever seen the sea took exception to the new tax with a ferocity that only gained by having to be bottled up during the "Eleven Years' Tyranny."

Charles who had inherited none of his father's guile and ability to play off one power group against another proceeded to drive the Scots into the enemy camp. His subjects north of the Border could raise little anger at the way in which Charles was treating his English landowning subjects; when Charles came to foist his religious ideas on a hardened Presbyterian nation, his subjects were literally up in arms and a Scottish army camped menacingly in the north of England.

Charles was eventually forced to call his Westminster Parliament again. It was the last time he was to do so, for the Parliament impeached all Charles' advisors and set about destroying the instruments of his tyranny.

Charles tried some heavy handed tactics to imprison the five key members who fled from the House by boat and the political situation drifted slowly with the relentlessness of a Greek tragedy into Britain's bitterest Civil War, culminating in the defeat of the Royalist forces by the seemingly invincible Oliver Cromwell and the surrender of the King to the Scots. He refused to accept the reality of a Presbyterian Scotland, was handed over to the Parliamentary forces and, after two years of fruitless negotiations in which Charles refused to yield on the basic principles of his Church and his Monarchy, the execution took place of the crowned King of the Scots and King of England.

John Hay
c. 1580-1636

—a faithful servant rewarded

The concept of a Fife playboy may be a difficult one to envisage. When you learn a little about John Hay, it will be easier.

John Hay, born at Wester Pitcorthy in the Fife parish of Carnbee around the year 1580, features on the Barbados stamps commemorating the granting of the charter by Charles

I in 1627. He is the recipient of the largesse, just one of many he received from the first two Stuarts to rule England.

Lord Hay, landed and titled in Scotland, formed part of the band of courtiers which came south with James in 1603. He accumulated honours south of the Border as befitted a loyal servant, becoming Lord Hay of Sauley in the English peerage and representing his monarch as ambassador to the Court of France and to the Emperor Ferdinand II. He was admitted to the Privy Council as Viscount Doncaster and in 1622 became the first Earl of Carlisle. He made sure of his favours continuing beyond the reign of James VI and I, when he played a leading part in the marriage negotiations between the future Charles I and his bride Henrietta Maria, daughter of Henri IV of France. Charles' gratitude for his part in finding him the wife he deeply loved was reflected in the ceding to Carlisle of the rights to develop Barbados. (The records suggest, however, that Charles gave it to yet another courtier before the death of John Hay.) Early in his career in England, Hay married a rich heiress and this, coupled with frequent hand-outs from his monarch, allowed him to carry out a sumptuous one-man campaign to dispel the widely-held image of the Scot as a tight-fisted, dour spoilsport.

His banquets, invariably held to impress and motivate someone who could be of use to him, were the most lavish ever seen in Britain. One observer noted an attendant of the King at one such banquet "eat a whole pye, reckoned to my Lord at £10, being composed of ambergris, magisterial of pearl, musk etc." The extravagance had to be seen to be believed. It reached the stage where guests came into the banqueting room and moved among the displayed foods and sweetmeats, admiring the silver and gold and the originality and appearance of the dishes. By the time they were ready to sit down the meal would be cold, so the Earl would serve an exact duplicate of the original food, hot and ready to enjoy!

At the end of a life of great extravagance and high living, John Hay died in 1636 with little to show for the favours bestowed by two monarchs. Lord Clarendon summed him up thus: "After having spent in a very jovial life £400,000 which upon strict computation he received from the Crown, he left not a house nor an acre of land to be remembered by."

John Murray, Earl of Dunmore 1732-1809

—linking the Bahamas with the States

When the Bahamas decided to mark the US Bicentenary with a set of stamps commemorating the long links between the two countries, they came up with a happy symbol of that link: John Murray, Earl of Dunmore, had been not only Governor of the Bahamas in the late eighteenth century but had previously been Governor of New York and Virginia.

The Earl appears, resplendent in two different tartans, in a fine portrait by Sir Joshua Reynolds which hangs in the National Gallery of Scotland. This portrait did duty both as the origination of the Bahamas stamp and as a loan to the USA during their own celebrations.

John Murray was born at Taymount near Stanley in Perthshire in 1732 and, with his background, picked the Jacobite side in the stirring events that were to accompany his youth. He was page to Prince Charles at the big social functions at Perth and Edinburgh, when the Prince was enjoying his early winning streak. In the sad years after Culloden, John Murray must have made a slow come back. He became Fourth Earl of Dunmore in 1756 and subsequently became part of the Scottish representation in Westminster as one of the elected peers. In 1770-1771 he was Governor of New York and later, until 1775, Governor of Virginia. With the colonies shaking off the need for British Governors, he returned to Britain, eventually crossing the Atlantic again as Governor of the Bahamas. He died in 1809.

The link between USA and Bahamas seems a neat one. In reality, it would have been difficult to find a man less suitable to commemorate the colonies' independence, for John Murray had fought tooth and nail to prevent it.

He took his responsibilities as Governor of Virginia very seriously. This, the jewel in the British Empire, had to be defended from attack without and treachery within and Murray had no doubts about his rôle. He stoutly defended the Western frontiers, in 1774 sending a force of 3000 men to stamp out an uprising among the Shawnee Indians in what was known as Lord Dunmore's War. He was no less decisive in meeting what he saw to be attacks from within his domain of Virginia. Rash, autocratic and aggressive, he had no sympathy with any attempts by the Virginia Assembly to express "revolutionary sentiments." In 1772, 1773 and 1774, at the first rumblings of such sentiments, he dissolved the gathering. When matters seemed to be developing along more serious tracks, he confiscated all the gunpowder in Virginia!

His efforts to strangle revolution were fruitless and he was forced to withdraw ignominiously to the safety of a British warship. Even then he plotted to enlist the aid of black slaves (with the offer freedom) and Red Indians (with the offer of land) in the cause of George III! He was eventually forced out of North America, leaving as his parting shot a full-scale bombardment of Norfolk.

"And so," sums up Feste at the end of *Twelfth Night,* "the whirligig of times brings in his revenges"— and the ghosts of the Virginian freedom fighters will surely smile wryly at the choice of the 4th Earl of Dunmore to celebrate the 200th anniversary of their victory.

Thomas Douglas, Earl of Selkirk 1771-1820

—the benevolent aristocrat

In the 1780s, the youngest son of a Scottish aristocrat was attending a social gathering in Paris, when someone mentioned to him that there was another Scot present, John Paul Jones. The teenage Thomas Douglas could hardly believe his ears and insisted on meeting the flamboyant bogey-man of Britain. The reason was more than a boy's natural desire to say he had spoken to the great US Commodore; Thomas Douglas had been a small child in the family home at St Mary's when in 1777 Jones' men had invaded and taken the family silver. Jones had gallantly returned the silver to the Countess after hostilities so there could hardly have been any rancour between the two who met by chance in that Paris salon.

Thomas Douglas was a dutiful and sensitive young man and in 1792 he made a trip which would eventually bring him, like John Paul Jones, fame in North America and a place in this book. He went to visit the Highlands, not for any reasons of family or property ties—there were none—but "by a warm interest in the fate of the natives." He was appalled by the misery being caused in remote and crofting communities as families were being turned out by ruthless landlords. He was convinced that the answer lay in planned emigration.

In 1799, he acquired the means to do something about that vision, when on the death of the last of his six brothers, he succeeded to the lands and the title of 4th Earl of Selkirk.

He had his attention drawn to the potential of the Red River valley, a fertile area of the territory which in theory at least belonged to the Hudson Bay Company. His first venture, however, did not involve that region. In 1802, the Earl masterminded an exodus of Highlanders, some 800 in all, to what is now Prince Edward Island. The colony proved viable and there are today proud descendents of that very successful colonisation.

The Earl, active at home and in London as one of Scotland's sixteen peers elected as representatives to the Westminster Parliament, still hankered after a larger colony on the Red River, and when in 1810 the stock of the Hudson Bay Company dropped to rock bottom as a result of the continuing Napoleonic Wars, the Earl bought up enough of it to give him control. He set aside 45,000,000 acres of land in the Red River area and designated it the site of a colony. In 1811, the first batch of pioneers set sail from Stornoway under Miles McDonell. They wintered on the Hudson Bay, withstood the hardships of months which were painfully cold even by that territory's standards and eventually progressed to the settlement where they set up Forts Douglas and Daer, Selkirk's family names.

The battle to establish the colony was a bitter one. The North West Fur Company, rivals to the trade of the Hudson Bay Company, regarded the newcomers as provocative intruders. The mixture of fraud and apathy on the part of some of the Earl's agents, accidents and appalling weather, obstruction and sheer armed aggression on the part of North West Fur, slowly poisoned the little colony despite heroic resistance from McDonell and his men. Buildings were burnt, crops were destroyed, supplies intercepted. Selkirk appealed for military protection; he carried the battle to the law courts where friends and relatives of North West Fur shareholders gave him less than justice. Selkirk was fined. Disillusioned, he returned to Europe, a man who had lost a fortune in a wholly philanthropic cause. He died at Pau in France on 8 April 1820 and never knew just how well he had laid the foundations of modern Manitoba.

Ironically, a year after his death, the Hudson Bay Company

and North West Fur merged and resolved to forget the past—
and that included the 4th Earl of Selkirk.

Her Majesty Queen Elizabeth the Queen Mother

—affectionately entitled "Queen Mum"

In the round of post-war visits to bind anew the nations of the
British Commonwealth, King George VI and his Queen came
in 1947 to South Africa and to a corner of that extensive and
beautiful dominion that had no love for the British Royal
family. The great White Train, gleaming in ivory and gold and
fully a third of a mile long, had pulled into the station of
Swellendam, the longest train ever to be seen there. In the
heart of nationalist republican Afrikaner territory, the Royal
visitors had no right to expect the sort of frenzied welcome that
had greeted them elsewhere. Moving along the line of local
worthies, the Queen came to an old farmer, a veteran of the
Boer War, renowned for his aggressive stance to all things
British. His exact words were not recorded by the attendant
press correspondents who had preceded the Royal family in the
special Pilot Train. But the gist of his words was clear: he did
not relish being pushed about by London and could never
forgive the English for their treatment. The Queen replied: "I
understand perfectly; we feel the same in Scotland."

Elizabeth Bowes-Lyon was born somewhere in the south of
England on 4 August 1900. The exact spot is at the moment a
matter of some conjecture as there is a possibility that her
father, the 14th Earl of Strathmore, may have absentmindedly
given the wrong address when registering her birth. The actual
place is totally unimportant as she has throughout her eighty

years been considered a Scot, even if her aristocratic background made it necessary to be born in England.

In 1923 she married Albert, Duke of York, after what most observers have claimed was a greater number of proposals than Royalty is used to making. After fourteen years of marriage and the birth of two daughters, Elizabeth and Margaret Rose, the Duke and Duchess of York became, on the dramatic abdication of Edward VIII, King and Queen of the United Kingdom and heads of a world-wide Empire.

It was the beginning of a long spell for Elizabeth at the centre of attention. Elizabeth, as Queen and later Queen Mother, performed her task with charm and distinction, acquiring the unofficial title of "Queen Mum" as a sign of the affection in which she is held.

Despite the wealth and glitter that goes with majesty, Queen Elizabeth the Queen Mother still faced a series of personal crises. The accession to the throne, in the bitter context of a confused and at that time little understood abdication, was traumatic. Albert had not been trained or even prepared for the responsibilities that were handed on to him. His shy nature, and his embarrassing stammer were distinct handicaps that his young wife had done much to overcome. No matter what had been achieved for the Duke of York, however, it had to be improved upon for the new King. The task was an unnerving one, and that the King emerged with the popularity he did was due in no small measure to the redoubtable Elizabeth.

Barely had the abdication affair died down than King George and Queen Elizabeth were at the head of a nation at war. The way in which the couple stuck to the task—and to Buckingham Palace—in the face of the London bombings brought home to the people again the high sense of duty and involvement of the Royal family; and in the post-war reconstruction of Britain and of the Empire the Queen, communicative, approachable and charming played an important part.

Tragedy and family crisis struck again with the early death of George VI, and the Queen came through the transition from wife of the King to mother of the Queen with all the resilience her people had come to expect. The official, but not the personal, mourning was ended with her first official visit as Queen Mother to Scotland as Colonel of the Black Watch, and she was off on an astonishing round of public engagements.

In the late 1950s, the two people to whom this book is dedicated were walking along a deserted back-street in Cambridge when they saw coming towards them a large respectable limousine, a standard fluttering, moving as slowly as if the empty pavements were lined with throngs. The Queen Mother was on her way to an unannounced appointment. The man, older than her, and the woman, a dozen years younger, stood and waved and received in return a cheerful wave and a resplendent smile and the limousine passed on. Today, at the drop of a mention of the Royal family, Cambridge or even limousines, those two people, children both of miners and born and bred in the town of Aneurin Bevan and Michael Foot, will tell the tale and relive the glow. That, to the despair of Marxists and Trotskyites, is what the Queen Mum is all about.

MORE
GREAT
SCOTS

L

William Clark Cowie 1849-1910

—a resourceful adventurer who became Number One

Peter Orr, his seafaring days coming to end, had an idea, he would buy a vessel in Scotland and sail it out to Singapore where he knew he would find a ready market for the vessel and would turn in a handsome profit. He was, however, totally unable to find any seamen willing to crew the vessel, for Orr had set his sights on a tiny toy of a ship, the 14-ton steam-ship *Argyle*, built as a pleasure launch to ply the Clyde and little bigger than the tourist coaches which bowl along the lanes of Scotland today.

Eventually Orr managed to muster a cook and three crew members, whose ignorance of maritime matters may have made them susceptible to his persuasion. One of them was a young engineer from Arbroath who had come to Glasgow to seek his fortune and put to good use his recently acquired engineering know-how. His first job was Chief Engineer of *SS Argyle* and it was to set him off on a career which would bring him some fame, even more fortune and the distinction not only of getting on a postage stamp in his own lifetime but also of being the first Scot to be honoured in this way.

William Clark Cowie had been born in 1849 to Ann Leitch and her husband David Cowie, a yarn inspector in the little village of Friockheim to the north-west of Arbroath. Traditionally in Scotland, the first son of a marriage bears the name of the paternal grandfather; in young Cowie's case this was not possible, for David had been the illigitimate son of mill-worker Mary Cowie. The baby was named after a local businessman friend of David Cowie's.

The village of Friockheim (pronounced Freek-ham) had an interesting history. It had been established specifically to attract energetic go-ahead weavers, and the founder John Anson named the village from the existing Gaelic feature name of Friock plus the German ending -heim in memory of his early trading days in Germany. David Cowie worked in the mill now owned by Anson's son, who lived two doors away from the Cowies and after whom the couple's next son, Anson, would be named. David Cowie was to turn out a model product of the model village, a vigorous respected, self-improved businessman. Liberal in his politics and active in local culture. The three Cowie sons, William, Anson and Edward, were the beneficiaries of David Cowie's progress, receiving a fine education at Arbroath. William, the first to emerge from schooling and to look for a job, found himself aboard the strange little vessel which left Renfrew in 1870 to set sail for Singapore via the newly opened Suez Canal.

The voyage was, to no-one's surprise, eventful; and to everyone's surprise, successful. The *Argyle* got off to a fair start with the steam engines working for the first three days— although this period did include a near wrecking off the coast of Northern Ireland. The engines were not used for the rest of the five-month voyage.

Entering the Suez Canal, *Argyle* collided with a dredger anchored in Lake Timsa and sunk. In the words of a letter to *The Times*, "the happy-go-lucky" crew raised her and carried on in the vague direction of Singapore. At Aden, the vessel went aground on a sand-bank and the crew were reduced to removing the propellors in order to get off. The *Argyle*, five months after she left Renfrew, bobbed into Singapore harbour, with five half-starved Scots ready to be saved from death.

The rest of Orr's plan worked out well. The pleasure craft was sold to the Sultan of an offshore island—and Cowie, appointed as Chief Engineer in his first post ever, became

Admiral of the Sultan's fleet for his second. Promotion was obviously going to be a speedy matter for young William.

After such a voyage, it would be difficult to find life in the East anything other than an anti-climax, but Cowie made certain it would not be. He established a trading company which worked out of Labuan on Borneo, indulging in gun-running to the beleaguered Sulu islanders who were trying hard to avoid becoming Spanish. This won him the support and friendship of the Sultan of Sulu and some valuable trading concessions. The former led him to play an important part in the establishment of British influence in Borneo while the latter led to the discovery and purchase of coal resources at Muara. The tide appeared to be running well for William Cowie and he returned to Arbroath to bring back his brothers, Anson to teach at Singapore School and Edward, a sad loss to the cricket fields of Angus, to help run his business.

The Cowie story is not an easy one to unravel, but what seems certain is that he lost the battle for control of North Borneo to the British North Borneo Company, established in 1881 and destined to be the most durable of the nineteenth-century chartered companies through which Britain directed her overseas influence.

Cowie was, however, a man who could snatch victory out of defeat, even after that defeat had been acknowledged by everyone else. He sold his mining rights to the great Rajah Brook, British ruler of Sarawak, and returned to Scotland a wealthy man. After a lengthy holiday on home territory he went off to the source of power, London, and proceeded to take control of the British North Borneo Company as the man who knew more about Borneo than anyone else, and who was really behind their company's success in Borneo. He rose to the Board, to the post of Managing Director and then to that of Chairman. He returned to meet the men who had upstaged him in Borneo—as their boss.

He re-established his undoubtedly good relations with the rulers and natives of the area. "He was," commented one admirer, "a welcome guest where others could not land without risking their lives." His plans were grandiose, and despite his assertion of intimate knowledge of Borneo, based on a large fiction. His knowledge of the interior, through which he planned to build a railway at a cost of £5000, was non-existent as were the hosts of friendly hardworking natives which he claimed were waiting to help lay the tracks. Bringing in Chinese labour—and defending the project against the real inhabitants of the interior, a small number of nasty cannibals—upped the cost to £20,000. The autocratic Cowie steamrollered through this and other proposals without any real opposition. By the turn of the century he was in full control, the real ruler of British North Borneo, and in 1909 featured at the right hand of the Sultan of Sulu on the territory's stamp.

Within a year he was dead. He went to Germany for an operation for an unspecified "internal malady" and died at Bad Neuheim on 14 September 1910. He was buried at Charlton Cemetery in London. The list of mourners, sprinkled with titles, and the subsequent publication of his will in which he left more than £50,000, underlined the achievement of William Clark Cowie in converting courage and resourcefulness into success.

Helen Bartholomew born 1889

—the Sultan and I

In 1921, the Sultan of Johore presented Edinburgh Zoo with a magnificent pair of Malay tigers. The populace of the capital city were enthralled and the Royal Zoological Society of Scotland, after the deprivations of the Great War, was ecstatic. In its annual report, it was moved to describe the gift as the finest of the year or indeed of any other year and announced that the Sultan had been made an Honorary Fellow of the Society.

Less than ten years later, on 1 October 1930, the Sultan, Sir Ibrahim, received something quite unusual from Scotland—a bride. On that date, at the Princes Row Registry Office in London, he married Helen Bartholomew and in 1935 when Johore issued a postage stamp depicting the couple in honour of the fifth wedding anniversary, she became the first lady Scot to appear on a postage stamping—pipping Her Majesty Queen Elizabeth the Queen Mother by a couple of years.

Helen Bartholomew was born at 10 Belgrave Street, Glasgow in December 1889, the daughter of John and Catherine Bartholomew. Her father was a master sawmaker from Stirlingshire.

Young Helen married William Brockie Wilson, a doctor, born in Johore to Scottish parents and educated in Edinburgh. The Johore birthplace was no coincidence as it was indeed a link that was to lead ultimately to that 1930 marriage. Dr Wilson was the personal physician to the Sultan—a post which seems to have been the preserve of Scots over the years. Helen returned with him to that exotic tip of the Malay peninsula.

The marriage ended—perhaps with the death of William Wilson—and Helen, Mrs Wilson, returned to Britain. When the Sultan sent some of his sons to boarding school, he renewed the acquaintance with Mrs Wilson, asking her to keep a motherly eye on the boys, especially during the vacations. He visited them on a few occasions and Helen's relationship to the boys turned from a "motherly" one to a step-motherly one with the wedding in 1930.

The marriage lasted for nearly ten years, but broke up in the late 1930s, with the couple parting amicably and the Sultan generous in his gifts and allowances. Helen Bartholomew Wilson, now Lady Ibrahim, returned briefly to her family, at that time living in Cambuslang, but then went south to spend the rest of her days in London, undisputed holder of the title of the first lady Scot on a stamp.

Unless of course one remembers that Britannia, a familiar device on so many of the British Empire's early stamps, was modelled on a well-known Scottish beauty at the Court of King Charles II.. . .

Jim Clark 1936-1968

—the farmer who was the world's best driver

On 7 April 1968, the accident occurred. There was nothing to suggest it could possibly happen. The race was a minor one— the German Formula II event at Hockenheim. Neither the car, a 1600cc Lotus Ford, nor the driver, Jim Clark, should have been troubled by high speed on that section of the track. But the car ran completely out of control and the world had lost its greatest racing car driver.

Jim Clark, born at Duns, a charming Borders county town, went to school at Loretto Academy in Musselburgh and returned to the Borders to become a farmer.

He acted as a mechanic for his friend and neighbour, Ian Scott-Watson, a racing enthusiast who in 1956 gave Clark a go at the wheel in a practice race in the north of Scotland. Jim Clark was hooked and by the next season was driving in a few races. In 1958, he became part of the Border Reivers team which drove D-type Jaguars. He was spotted by the Aston-Martin squad and signed up. The Aston-Martin cars never really made it on the race circuits and Jim Clark went on loan to Lotus Formula III squad, driving in a works team after only two seasons. He progressed up to the Lotus Formula I team and in 1963 became the youngest ever driver to win the World Championship. From then on he mopped up awards and titles: OBE in 1964, World Champion again in 1965, first Briton to win the Indianapolis 500 (and first non-American for nearly 50 years). At the start of the 1968 season he won the South African Grand Prix to set a world record of 25 Grand Prix wins. The unexplained accident at Hockenheim made sure that he never finished the season.

"He was," said Juan Fangio, perhaps the only man to challenge Clark's pre-eminence, "the greatest driver there has ever been." He was mourned as more than just a champion, a charming, balanced superstar who, his wins notched up, would return after each season to the other half of his life, sheep-breeding in the Scottish hills.

It is appropriate that Jim Clark's successor in the hearts of British racing fans was fellow Scot Jackie Stewart, diminutive world champion who also featured on a stamp issued by the Gulf State of Ajman.

Arthur Whitten Brown 1886-1948

SIR JOHN ALCOCK, SIR ARTHUR WHITTEN BROWN
1919-1979
100 F
REPUBLIQUE DU NIGER

—knighted for landing in a bog

In 1919, a Vickers Vimy twin-engined biplane flopped wearily down in a glutinous bog in County Galway near the Atlantic battered west coast of Ireland. With such an unconventional landing spot, one would normally expect the navigator of the aeroplane to come in for some stick from his commanding pilot. On this occasion, both of them received knighthoods.

The pilot was Captain J. W. Alcock and his navigator Arthur Whitten Brown. They had made the first non-stop flight of the Atlantic starting from St Johns, Newfoundland and finishing up 16 hours and 27 minutes later in that Galway bog, having completed the crossing at an average speed of about 120 miles per hour.

The Scot involved was Arthur Brown, born in Glasgow to US parents on 23 July 1886. His parents, Arthur Brown and Emma Whitten, had been married in Pittsburg, Pennsylvania in 1884. He was given his father's name and his mother's family name was added. Brown, following in his father's footsteps, trained as an engineer at the famous Westinghouse plant in Manchester. He went to South Africa in 1912, but returned to fight in the First World War with the Manchester Regiment. He moved on to the Royal Flying Corps and later to the Royal Air Force. With the War barely out of their systems, Alcock and Brown decided to make an attempt to win the £10,000 offered by the *Daily Mail* for the first non-stop Transatlantic flight. They shared the prize.

Brown continued a career in engineering, but naturally did not manage to make the sort of headlines that greeted his 1919 venture. He worked as General manager of the Metropolitan-Vickers at Swansea and died there in 1948.

Sir David and Lady Isabel Gill

Sir David & Lady Gill at the Site of their Living Tent

Ascension Island 12p

Centenary of the visit of Professor Gill to Ascension Island

—the only husband-wife team to make it

In 1870, David Gill, son of an Aberdeen watchmaker, married Isabel, daughter of a farmer in the county. It was the only marriage in Scotland to produce a husband-and-wife team on a postage stamp.

David Gill, a bright lad even by Aberdeen standards, studied physical science at the local university under Scotland's greatest scientist, Clerk Maxwell. He left university and ran his father's clockmaking business for some time. He never lost his passion for the sciences, however, and worked in his own laboratory, grappling with the fascination of physics and chemistry. In 1863, at the age of twenty, he made a purchase which was to change his life: he bought a small telescope. In 1872, he turned his passion of astronomy into a full-time job, giving up his profitable clock-making business to take charge of Lord Lindsay's private observatory at Dunecht.

Gazing at stars was certainly no observatory-bound occupation for David Gill. In 1874, he went off to Mauritius to observe Venus—his upbringing came in useful when he came to transport fifty chronometers down to Greenwich for accurate calibration and then off to the Indian Ocean for the accurate observations.

On Mauritius, he met the Khedive of Egypt's chief of military staff who succeeded in getting Gill to set up the great national survey of Egypt. It is a country not short of landmarks and Gill set up his base-line alongside the Sphinx.

Work at Dunecht provided another diversion when its manager went off with his wife to Ascension in 1877, to set up a project to measure the distance of Mars and from that to calculate the distance of the sun. The experiences of the kindly and enthusiastic couple form the basis of the book *Six Months in Ascension—an Unscientific Account of a Scientific Expedition*—and Ascension issued a stamp to mark the centenary of the couple's visit.

In 1879, Gill was appointed as Her Majesty's Astronomer at the Cape of Good Hope and over the next twenty-eight years built up the observatory to a fine, well-equipped centre of astronomy.

In his work, Sir David, as he became in 1900, was a systematic astronomer, with, thanks to his upbringing as scientist and craftsman, considerable skill in the design and coordination of the astronomer's hardware. In private life, the Gills were by all accounts a charming, delightful couple. They had no children of their own, but brought up three orphan sons of David Gill's younger brother.

Alexander Selkirk
1676-1721

—immortality under someone else's name

In 1712 at Largo, a cluster of houses huddled around one of those tiny Fife harbours, the congregation of the kirk was interrupted by the arrival back home of its prodigal son, Alexander Selkirk. He could hardly have expected a welcome; after all, he had run off to sea seventeen years earlier to escape having to answer a charge of indecent behaviour in church. During his brief return in 1701, he had been called to answer to the congregation for brawling with his brothers. This time, however, there was a difference; he had left, notorious in Largo, he returned famous throughout the country. And he had chosen a very unusual means of achieving fame.

His buccaneering had in 1704 taken him to serve in the "fleet" of William Dampier. Selkirk had had a quarrel with the captain of his ship, one Tom Stradling, and had asked to be put ashore on the island of Juan Fernandez rather than continue to serve under such a captain. (Tradition also maintains that Selkirk had claimed the ship was unseaworthy and had asked to put ashore to avoid the inevitable destruction, which did in fact occur.)

Selkirk lived alone on the island until he was picked up by another vessel. He had eked out an enterprising existence on the island, building huts, living from the milk and meat of the many goats that lived on the island and kitting himself out in a very distinctive suit of goatskin.

On his return to England his tale appeared in the *Englishman*. Several years later, the writer Daniel Defoe, whose knowledge of Scotland had been gathered while spying for the English government in the years around the Act of Union, retold the story, thickly camouflaged as fiction, going to great lengths to concoct a name of Robinson Crusoe. Alexander Selkirk had achieved immortality—but achieved it under another name.

Selkirk lived the life of an eccentric recluse back in Largo, went off to sea again and died in 1721 as mate of *HMS Weymouth*, undoubtedly the strangest Scot to figure in this book.

Denis Law
born 1940

—in the hall of footballing fame

In 1955, Huddersfield Football Club took delivery of a new investment, a fifteen-year-old footballer from the northernmost outpost of League football, Aberdeen. It was his first signing so they had not paid much—and at first glance Denis Law did not look as if any more money would have been justified. Frail of stature, hair fair and floppy, he had clearly not been designed for the hurly-burly of professional football. His thick spectacles, designed to sort out a squint, were more in keeping with someone at the ground to collect autographs rather than there for training. But appearances were deceptive.

Within three years, Denis Law was collecting his first cap for Scotland, the youngest player to do so for two generations. Two seasons later he was signed by Manchester City for a record £55,000 fee; four seasons later he was moving to Manchester United for £116,000 having had his market value and international fame boosted by two seasons with Gigi Peronace's prestigious Turin club. Of that £116,000 signing on fee, United's manager Matt Busby commented: "It was still a bargain". And so it proved.

Denis Law, impetuous craftsman, crowd-puller and embodiment of the Scotsman's footballing dream, illuminated British and Scottish football for many years. In 1980, when Nicaragua came to produce one of its characteristic long series of footballing greats, Denis Law featured in tandem with another unique European player, Franz Beckenbauer. Other Scots have appeared on stamps associated with World Cup scenes, notably Bruce Rioch and Pat Crerand. Only Law has been singled out for personal recognition in this way. And if any modern Scot was to be so honoured, few of his countrymen would disagree with Nicaragua's choice.